THE JOY OF JESUS/ CRUSHING ALL OTHER IDOLS

ANDREW ZINK

Copyright © 2024 by Andrew Zink

All rights are reserved, and no part of this publication may be reproduced, distributed, or transmitted in any manner, whether through photocopying, recording, or any other electronic or mechanical methods, without the explicit prior written permission of the publisher. This restriction applies to any form or means of reproduction or distribution.

Exceptions to this rule include brief quotations that may be incorporated into critical reviews, as well as certain other noncommercial uses that are allowed by copyright law. Any such usage must adhere to the specified conditions and permissions outlined by the copyright holder.

Book Design by HMDPUBLISHING

CONTENTS

01. Where Are You? 4
02. Never Enough 8
03. Chasing The Wind 12
04. Staying High 16
05. Trying And Dying For Joy 21
06. A Joyful Mind 27
07. Today Is The Day 31
08. The Race For Joy 34
09. Choose Joy 37
10. Biblical Joy 40
11. Man's Chief End 44
12. A Want That Never Ends 47
13. A Different Kind Of Joy 50
14. Fighting For Joy Through Faith 53
15. Joy In The Midst Of Suffering 56
16. Finding Joy in the Word of God 59
17. Finding Joy in the Holy Spirit 64
18. Crush Your Idol/s Before It Crushes You 71
19. The Joy of Prayer: A Heartfelt Conversation 79
20. Don't Let The Devil Steal Your Joy 83
21. Finding Joy In The Presence Of The Father 90
22. Joy In Having The Mind Of Christ 95
23. The Joy Of Never Giving Up 100
24. I Will Fear No Evil God Is With Me 106
25. Rejoice! Again I Say Rejoice! 110
26. Stir Yourself Up With The Joy Of The Lord 114
27. I Can Do All Things Through Christ 121
28. Eternal Joy 126
Conclusion 127

CHAPTER 1
WHERE ARE YOU?

"Let us occupy ourselves entirely in knowing God. The more we know Him, the more we will desire to know Him. As love increases with knowledge, the more we know God, the more we will truly love Him. We will learn to love Him equally in times of distress or in times of great joy."

Brother Lawrence

There is no greater joy than to know Christ

> There is no greater joy than to know Christ

I don't know about you, but I am so tired of feeling down and out. I am tired of having to go to war with myself just to get up in the morning. I am tired of believing all the lies from the devil and his demons that constantly run through my mind day in and day out. And frankly, I am just tired of myself. I am so far gone that I don't feel like even God can help me. Is He even real? Why does he feel so far away? If He is near, why is He not helping me? Does any of this sound familiar to you?

If so, please keep on reading. We may not like to admit it, but unless you are a "super saint," I believe that has been all of us at some point or another in our times of tribulation. But we definitely were not the first ones to feel this way. Just like Adam and Eve in the garden of Eden, in times of trial, we feel naked and ashamed, so lost and vulnerable. But yet, in a gentle yet omnipotent voice, we hear in the shadows.

> Where are you?

"Where are you?" He answered, "I heard you in the garden, and I was afraid because I was naked; so I hid." And he said, "Who told you that you were naked? Have you eaten from the tree that I commanded you not to eat from?" Genesis 3:10-11 (NIV).

Of course, God knew very well where Adam was and why he was naked. God didn't ask for information; He asked for confirmation. And to some of us who are caught up in our own trials, troubles, and tribulation, I believe He is asking us that same question today.

"Where are you? Who told you that you were naked?" So, as we will see in the chapters to come, God didn't walk away from us. We originally walked away from Him. But we will find that even though we did so, not only does God love us with an everlasting love, but He also says,

"For I am jealous for you with godly jealousy. For I have betrothed you to one husband that I may present you as a chaste virgin to Christ." 2 Corinthians 11:2.

> Although we may "feel" God is not with us, we can know for certain that He is.

We will also find that although we may "feel" He is not with us, we can know for certain that He is. And I am not just talking about knowing intellectually in our minds, but rather letting this ultimate truth drive deep down in our hearts so much so that we know that we know He is with us, and He promises He will never leave us or forsake us.

In Hebrew, the word for "know" is Yada. Yada indicates a combination of close, warm, and even passionate intimacy. It can also combine head knowledge with that intimacy to produce an edge in a person's life. This edge enables a person to trust God and perceive what He is doing.

That is the kind of knowing we are so desperately yearning for and so desperately need. As we start this journey together, I want you to imagine God walking in the cool of the day with you and asking you that same question he asked Adam. A question that not only snaps us back to reality but far more importantly into the arms of The One who loves you so much so that He made the first, the last, and the ultimate move to reach you! Then, you will be able to answer that question with full conviction, knowing that we have a God who not only says He is with you but "wants" and "is" with you to eternity and beyond. So "where are you and who said that you were naked?"

As I close this chapter, I'd like to share a quote from the great, late theologian J.I. Packer.

"Knowing God is a relationship calculated to thrill a man's heart." "To know that nothing happens in God's world apart from God's will may frighten the godless, but it stabilizes the saints." "Your faith will not fail while God sustains it; you are not strong enough to fall away while God is resolved to hold you."

I want us to "Yada" God so much that we know who we are, we know where we've been, and we know where we are going. But most importantly, we know the One who is more than enough. We already know a lot about God. But I beseech you to come with me on this journey to truly "know" (Yada) God and enter the joy of Jesus! Let us begin with a Psalm and prayer of King David. As we begin to go back to the garden,

"Turn to me and be gracious to me, for I am lonely and afflicted. Relieve the troubles of my heart and free me from my anguish. Look on my affliction and my distress and take away all my sins. See how numerous are my enemies and how fiercely they hate me! Guard my life and rescue me; do not let me be put to shame, for I take refuge in you. May integrity and uprightness protect me because my hope, LORD, is in you. Deliver me, O God, from all my troubles! Psalm 25:16-22 NIV (emphasis added).

> **JOY BUILDER TIP:**
>
> Sit down or lay down in your bed. Turn off or silence your phone if possible and try to noise out any distractions. Say a prayer or ask God a petition and then literally just sit there in silence for as long as you feel comfortable. I know in our world today with so many distractions it is hard to sit still. But I guarantee you the more you just sit quiet in the presence of the Almighty your joy will significantly increase. There is no one anywhere ever who is better to spend time with than our Creator

For more resources to help you win the war for your mind and to help you find true joy please visit andrewzink-setyourmind.com

CHAPTER 2
NEVER ENOUGH

"We are far too easily pleased "

> **I**t would seem that Our Lord finds our desires not too strong, but too weak. We are half-hearted creatures, fooling about with drink and sex and ambition when infinite joy is offered to us, like an ignorant child who wants to go on making mud pies in a slum because he cannot imagine what is meant by the offer of a holiday at the sea. We are far too easily pleased. "— C.S. Lewis.

Whether we'd like to admit it or not, every decision we make and everything we ever do is based on whether that next move brings us happiness or not. People don't climb Mount Everest out of boredom. Nor do people caught in addictions use drugs to make them feel miserable. Of course, in the end, it turns on them like a viper. But, needless to say, anything and everything we do is something that we hope will bring us happiness. We all long for it. We all search for it in bars, stars, cars, and even Mars. But it seems that the more we search for it in all the wrong places, ironically, the sadder we become. But what if there was something, or rather Someone, that is greater than happiness yet at the same time brings a joy that nothing in this world could ever bring? A joy unspeakable. So much so that when you encounter It, your life will never be the same? Someone who says to you, "Cast all your cares on Him because He cares for you," and pleads with you,

"Come to me, all you who are weary and burdened, and I will give you rest. Take my yoke upon you and learn from me, for I am gentle and humble in heart, and you will find rest for your souls." — Matthew 11:28-30.

I don't know about you, but I am tired of "looking for love in all the wrong places." I am tired of never being satisfied no matter how hard I try. I am tired of feeling so empty when I know I was created for so much more. I know if you have picked up this book that you feel the same way as well. Well, the good news is I have the answer to all our problems! Actually, He is the Answer, and He has us.

I invite you to come with me on this journey to find the joy of Jesus, and I guarantee your life will never be the same! When we have finally come to the end of ourselves and realize that nothing in this world is ever enough to fully satisfy our souls, it is when Jesus comes in and says, "I am more than enough, and I will never leave you nor forsake you!" It's been said that God wants us holy but not happy.

I firmly disagree. In fact, I don't believe you can be holy without being happy and vice versa. But make no mistake, as Jesus promised,

"In this world, you will have troubles." But that is not the end of that verse. "But be of good cheer (happy), I have overcome the world!"

And as James 1:2-4 states,

"Consider it pure joy, my brothers and sisters, whenever you face trials of many kinds, because you know that the testing of your faith produces perseverance. Let perseverance finish its work so that you may be mature and complete, not lacking anything."

> When" trials come consider it joy because we know God is working on our faith through them.

James is not by any means saying be thankful "for" the trials but rather "when" trials come consider it joy because we know God is working on our faith through them. That's the joy and happiness I am speaking of here. That no matter what comes our way in every circumstance, through it all, we can have true joy. Like the apostle Paul says,

"I have learned in whatever situation therewith to be content. I know how to be abased and how to abound. Everywhere and in all things. I am instructed both to be full and to be hungry. Both to abound and suffer need. I can do all things through Christ who strengthens me." — Philippians 4:11-13.

Of course, we have our adversary who came to kill, steal, and destroy, but we have One that is greater than all Who says," He came so we may have and enjoy our lives abundantly." Let this be the day that the devil kills and steals no more. He can take away everything, but he can never take away our Jesus and what we have in Him! The devil knows he can never steal our salvation but will do everything in his power to make us miserable down here on our way to heaven. So, one of the biggest black eyes we can ever give him is living the rest of our short lives down here in the joy of Jesus! I'd like to end this chapter with a quote from the late great music legend Johnny Cash and a prayer to strengthen our walk.

> "There is nothing in this world more satisfying than God"

"I have tried drugs and a little of everything else. And there is nothing in the world more soul-satisfying than God. It takes a real man to live for God – a lot more than to live for the devil. Everything I have and everything I do is now given completely to Jesus Christ. He is the only way to Heaven."

And I will add, the only way to true and everlasting joy! The joy of Jesus!

Dear Lord, forgive me when I've looked to everything and anyone else for the joy that only you can bring. I ask you with all my heart that you impart your joy to me like never before so I can live and love like you like never before! In the most joyful Name of all. The name of Jesus. Amen Selah

JOY BUILDER TIP:
Pick one of your favorite verses from the Bible or one specific to your current situation. If able take a short or long walk and meditate, mull over, ponder and even speak that verse until it sits deep in your heart. You can do this as often as needed and can pick a different verse or use the same verse every time

CHAPTER 3
CHASING THE WIND

I have seen all the things that are done under the sun; all of them are meaningless, a chasing after the wind.
Ecclesiastes 1:14.

> As long as we keep digging our own cisterns, broken cisterns that hold no water. Instead of bathing in the living water, our souls will never be satisfied!

I just love how the Bible is perfectly perfect! There is no better way to describe chasing our worldly pursuits and pleasures than "chasing the wind." Honestly, think about that for a second. Think about the last bad habit or addiction you had and thought, "I got it this time. If I just take enough of this or do enough of that, I will finally be happy. If I work 5 more hours this week or make ten thousand more dollars this month, that will be enough." Until we attain those things and find that it never is. And in the words of the Teacher, "that too is meaningless and chasing after the wind." As long as we keep digging our own cisterns, broken cisterns that hold no water. Instead of bathing in the living water, our souls will never be satisfied! One of the greatest tragedies to me in the Bible is when God literally did everything in His power to free the Israelites from their bondage in Egypt.

And God said, "You Take care lest you forget the Lord your God by not keeping his commandments and his rules and his statutes, which I command you today, lest, when you have eaten and are full and have built good houses and live in them, and when your herds and flocks multiply and your silver and gold is multiplied and all that you have is multiplied, then your heart be lifted up, and you forget the Lord your God, who brought you out of the land of Egypt, out of the house of slavery, who led you through the great and terrifying wilderness, with its fiery serpents and scorpions and thirsty ground where there was no water, who brought you water out of the flinty rock, who fed you in the wilderness with manna that your fathers did not know, that he might humble you and test you, do you good in the end. Beware lest you say in your heart, 'My power and the might of my hand have gotten me this wealth.' You shall remember the Lord your God, for it is he who gives you power to get wealth, that he may confirm his covenant that he swore to your fathers, as it is this day." Deuteronomy 8:11–18.

And forget about Him they did. The Israelites forgot, but God did not! 40 years later, wandering in the desert. We all know how the story goes. But we all know we have had our own deserts as well. Maybe not 40 years. Could be less or even more. But we all have either been, will eventually be, or are currently in the "desert" right now. But no matter whatever desert or hardships you may face, I want you to imagine God saying to you the same thing He said to the Israelites about not yet entering the promised land. "You have stayed long enough on this mountain." Deuteronomy 1:6. In the words of Tom Petty,

"It's time to move on, it's time to get going. What lies ahead, I have no way of knowing. But under my feet, baby, grass is growing. It's time to move on, time to get going."

I don't believe there has ever been or will ever be any man or woman in history who sought happiness by indulging in worldly pleasures more than King Solomon. I mean, this guy literally tried everything! As we read in Ecclesiastes 2:1-11, I said to myself,

"Come now, I will test you with pleasure to find out what is good." But that also proved to be meaningless. "Laughter," I said, "is madness. And what does pleasure accomplish?" I tried cheering myself with wine, and embracing folly—my mind still guiding me with wisdom. I wanted to see what was good for people to do under the heavens during the few days of their lives. I undertook great projects: I built houses for myself and planted vineyards. I made gardens and parks and planted all kinds of fruit trees in them. I made reservoirs to water groves of flourishing trees. I bought male and female slaves and had other slaves who were born in my house. I also owned more herds and flocks than anyone in Jerusalem before me.

I amassed silver and gold for myself and the treasure of kings and provinces. I acquired male and female singers, and a harem as well—the delights of a man's heart. I became greater by far than anyone in Jerusalem before me. In all this, my wisdom stayed with me. I denied myself nothing my eyes desired; I refused my heart no pleasure.

My heart took delight in all my labor, and this was the reward for all my toil. Yet when I surveyed all that my hands had done and what I had toiled to achieve, everything was meaningless, a chasing after the wind; nothing was gained under the sun.

Surprisingly, the list goes on. But I think we get the idea. And what we know from history Solomon was said to be the richest man ever. He would make Warren Buffet look like Warren who? Can money buy you nice things? Yes. Can it buy you happiness? I would firmly say absolutely not. Possibly little moments of temporal happiness. But never true lasting eternal happiness. The Preacher goes onto say. Those who love money will never have enough. How meaningless to think that wealth brings true happiness!

Ecclesiastes 5:10

> All the money in the world couldn't pay for the true joy that we so long to have.

We have all heard it said that money is or has power. Money definitely has the power to buy you nice things. But it doesn't have the power from keeping those things from having power over you. Money even has the power to buy people. Like wives and husbands. We see it all the time. But money does not have the power to make that wife or husband love you for who you are rather than for what you have. So does money have power? Kind of but not the kind of power we want that can only come through the Holy Spirit! I believe it was Pastor Alistair Begg who once said, "If you have a penny in your pocket, you are richer than John D Rockefeller. Why? Cause Rockefeller is dead!" All the money in the world couldn't pay for the true joy that we so long to have. Why? Cause it's free! And it's right there for the taking! Jesus said,

> "I have told you these things so that My joy and delight may be in you, and that your joy may be made full and complete and overflowing."
> **John 15:11(AMP)**

And the Father also promised that

> "He will show us the path of life. In His presence, there is fullness of joy. At His right hand are pleasures forevermore."
> **Psalm 16:11.**

Please don't settle one more day for these fleeting temporal pleasures that will never fill you. But rather soak yourself in the presence of The Almighty, and you will have eternal pleasures that will last forever!

JOY BUILDER TIP:

Lay or sit somewhere comfortable. Put on one of your favorite worship songs. And reflect on God's goodness and thank Him for all He's done and is doing in your life. Just like King David in the book of Psalms.

CHAPTER 4
STAYING HIGH

All Things are lawful for me, but not all things are helpful. All things are lawful for me, but I will not be dominated by anything".
1 Corinthians 6:12

I'm sure anyone familiar with drug addiction has heard the saying "chasing the dragon," which can truthfully be applied to any addiction or pleasure in life. I found a great definition of it on a website that says, "It is an expression given to the pursuit of the original or ultimate but unattainable high, which can lead to a dangerous spiral of legal and health consequences."

In other words, it is someone trying to feel as high as they were the first time they used. But anyone involved in addiction knows that will never happen. But it doesn't stop them from trying. As we know from John 8:44, the Bible says about Satan: "He was a murderer from the beginning and has nothing to do with the truth because there is no truth in him. When he lies, he speaks according to his own nature, for he is a liar and the father of lies." He is the ultimate deceiver. I believe one of his greatest strategies is to make us believe that we can truly find true happiness in worldly pleasures. Because as long as we believe that, it will keep us from going to the ultimate source of happiness, which, of course, is Jesus and His Word.

> As long as we keep believing worldly treasures will bring us true joy it will stop us from going to the Ultimate Source of happiness Either this Book will keep you from sin or sin will keep you from this Book."

It has been well said about the Bible that "either this Book will keep you from sin or sin will keep you from this Book." A great late friend of mine was a very famous blues legend who also had one of the most difficult lives I've known. He would always tell me about his past drug use, saying "He didn't get high. He stayed high." Until one day, walking down Sunset Blvd in California, where he came to the end of himself. He came across the great Saint Arthur Blessit, who literally carried the Cross around the world. He told my friend to "stop dropping uppers and downers and start picking up Matthew, Mark, Luke, and John." I'll never forget those words.

> "Stop dropping uppers and downers and start picking up Matthew, Mark, Luke, and John."

Probably one of the worst parts about addiction is that no matter how high you get, you will always come down. God made gravity for a reason. There is one addiction, however, that you can stay high on all the days of your life. That will bring everlasting joy. The effects of it are righteousness, peace, and joy in the Holy Spirit. Along with the fruit of the Spirit: love, joy, peace, forbearance, kindness, goodness, faithfulness, gentleness, and self-control. Against such things, there is no law (Galatians 5:22-23). That is being addicted to Christ.

Now, please don't get me wrong. I am in no way comparing our great Savior to a drug. Nor am I saying you can use and abuse Him like one. But I am saying that He wants us to want Him more than anything. "You will seek me and find me when you seek me with all your heart" (Jeremiah 29:13). And now to Him who is able to [carry out His purpose and] do superabundantly more than all that we dare ask or think [infinitely beyond our greatest prayers, hopes, or dreams], according to His power that is at work within us (Ephesians 3:20).

> You can literally never get enough of Jesus, yet at the same time, He is more than enough.

Even the Word itself uses the analogy of comparing drinking to the filling of the Holy Spirit: "Be not drunk with wine but be filled with the Holy Spirit" (Ephesians 5:18). So once again, I want to be clear. I am by no means calling our great God a drug. With that said, however, I do propose that we all become Christ addicts! You can literally never get enough of Jesus, yet at the same time, He is more than enough. If we love God with all our heart and with all our soul and with all our strength and with all our mind, and our neighbor as ourselves, we will never run dry of the living water!

We must fight the good fight with everything that is inside with the Holy Spirit's help to never give up on seeking God. To never turn back to our old ways. To run our race with great confidence and finally silence the roars of the devil! To take back what the enemy has stolen. To aim towards that heavenly prize and do whatever it takes to know the Lord and show The Lord to all! And not I but the Bible and God Himself promises that if you do this, being confident of this, that he who began a good work in you will carry it on to completion until the day of Christ Jesus (Philippians 1:6).

So let us turn from our worldly idols and temporal pleasures that are fleeting and will never satisfy our broken souls. And like my great friend said, "Let's not get high on Jesus, but let us stay high!" I'd like to end this chapter with a great, but sad and true poem I heard long ago that speaks of the misery and death of pursuing worldly pleasures. As you read, you can replace the word drugs with anything that is holding you back from true freedom and joy in Christ:

Hello, My name is DRUGS – I destroy homes, tear families apart, take your children, and that's just the start. I'm more costly than diamonds, more costly than gold, the sorrow I bring is a sight to behold. And if you need me, remember I'm easily found; I live all around you, in schools and in town. I live with the rich, I live with the poor, I live down the street, and maybe next door. My power is awesome; try me you'll see, but if you do, you may NEVER break free. Just try me once and I might let you go, but try me twice and I'll own your soul. When I possess you, you'll steal, cheat and lie. You do what you have to just to get high. The crimes you'll commit, for my narcotic charms will be worth the pleasure you'll feel in your arms. You'll lie to your mother, you'll steal from your Dad, when you see their tears you should feel bad. But you'll forget your morals and how you were raised, I'll be your conscience, I'll teach you my ways. I take kids from parents, and parents from kids, I turn people from God and separate friends. I'll take everything from you, your looks and your pride; I'll be with you always, right by your side. You'll give up everything...your family, your home...your friends, your money, then you'll be alone. I'll take and take until you've got nothing more to give. When I'm finished with you you'll be lucky to live. If you try me be warned this is no game, if given the chance I'll drive you insane.

I'll ravish your body, I'll control your mind, I'll own you completely; your soul will be mine. The nightmares I'll give you while lying in bed, the voices you'll hear from inside your head. The sweats, the shakes, the visions you'll see; I want you to know, these are all gifts from me. But when it's too late, and you'll know in your heart, that you are mine and we shall not part. You'll regret that you tried me, they always do, but you came to me, not I to you. You knew this would happen. Many times you were told, but you challenged my power, you chose to be bold.

You could have said no, and just walked away, If you lived your life over, what would you say? You knew this would happen, many times you were told. But you challenged my power and chose to be bold. Then when it's too late, you'll know in your heart that you are now mine -Till death us do part. I'll be your master, you'll be my slave, I'll even go with you, right to your grave.

So now that you've met me what will you do? Will you take it or leave it its all up to you. I can bring you more misery than mere words can tell, So come take my hand, I'll take you to hell

JOY BUILDER TIP:

Think of someone who God has put on your heart or someone maybe you don't get to see often. Either send them a text, give them a call and tell them how much you love them and how grateful you are for them or buy them a simple gift.

For more resources to help you win the war for your mind and to help you find true joy please visit andrewzinksetyourmind.com

CHAPTER 5
TRYING AND DYING FOR JOY

Rejoice in the Lord always; again I will say, rejoice.
Phillipians 4:4

Anytime I think of fighting for something you believe in, I am always reminded of the folktale of John Henry. From Wikipedia, John Henry was an African American freedman. He is said to have worked as a "steel-driving man"—a man tasked with hammering a steel drill into rock to make holes for explosives to blast the rock in constructing a railroad tunnel.

The story of John Henry is told in a classic blues folk song about his duel against a drilling machine. Another excerpt from Wikipedia from a man who stated that John Henry was not just a folk hero but a real person, and he goes on to say, "This man, known as Neal Miller, told me in plain words how he had come to the tunnel with his father at 17, how he carried water and drills for the steel drivers, how he saw John Henry every day, and, finally, all about the contest between John Henry and the steam drill.

"When the agent for the steam drill company brought the drill here," said Mr. Miller, "John Henry wanted to drive against it. He took a lot of pride in his work, and he hated to see a machine take the work of men like him.

"Well, they decided to hold a test to get an idea of how practical the steam drill was. The test went on all day and part of the next day.

"John Henry won. He wouldn't rest enough, and he overdid. He took sick and died soon after that." Whether folklore or not, I get chills every time I read that story. With all the technology we have today and advancements in science, let us not forget it is we the people who created them. But even more so, we were created by The Creator of all! Let us compare that steam drill to the flesh and John Henry as walking in The Spirit. In a way, a broken machine is like the flesh. It repetitively does the things we don't want it to do. But in this story, the machine would more represent Pride. It was supposed to be the best of the best, and nothing could stop it. Kind of reminds me of Satan before the fall

> *'I will ascend into heaven, I will exalt my throne above the stars of God; I will also sit on the mount of the congregation on the farthest sides of the north; I will ascend above the heights of the clouds, I will be like the Most High'*
> ***(Isaiah 14:12-14).***

By building the machine, they were looking for the easy way. It makes me think of Jesus' words in Matthew 7:13-14,

"Enter through the narrow gate. For wide is the gate, and the broad is the road that leads to destruction, and many enter through it. But small is the gate and narrow the road that leads to life, and only a few find it."

In the words of the Rocky 4 soundtrack,

"there ain't no easy way out. There ain't no shortcut home."

> "There ain't no easy way out. There ain't no shortcut home."

The Lord never promised us a trouble-free life, but He did promise us something far better, and that is freedom in Him. It is so easy to sin yet so hard sometimes to do what is right. As we continue to find the Joy of Jesus, I must warn you now that this will be a great fight. But make no mistake as we fight, we have the "Greatest Fighter" of all time on our side who has never lost one round of the match. Since the day of the tale of John Henry, they have built machines 10 times as fast as the one in the story. But on that day, the machine lost that fight. So, it is with us. The devil can come with his best tactics, his best mechanisms, and machines against us. But let us never forget that greater is

He who is in us than he who is in the world
(1 John 4:4).

> Not today devil, not any day anymore.

John Henry died that day after he beat that machine, but I guarantee that he went out with great joy and an integrity that says. You can bring your best. All your technologies, all your schemes, all your wicked ways. But not today devil, not any day anymore. And Jesus did the same thing for the Father and for us,

who for the joy that was set before him endured the cross, despising the shame, and is set down at the right hand of the throne of God"
(Hebrews 12:2).

Most people, when the death of a loved one comes, are comforted with the words of Jesus saying, "Well done, good and faithful servant." Please don't get me wrong. To hear those words from Jesus to us, nothing could compare. But there are some other words in Scripture that I so pray that all of us can say when we come to the end. And not in any prideful way whatsoever but rather knowing that through Christ we didn't waste one minute of this life He gave us. The words St Paul said near his departure.

I hav e fought the good fight, I have finished the race, and I have kept the faith. Now there is in store for me the crown of righteousness, which the Lord, the righteous Judge, will award to me on that day—and not only to me, but also to all who have longed for his appearing" (2 Timothy *4:6-8).*

There is no greater joy than to know the One who brings us joy. So today and every day, let us with great perseverance and strength fight for the joy of Jesus and bring it to as many people as possible. And even if like John Henry, we die by doing so, so be it. It would be worth every soul that we may win to Christ! And just like the Lord said to Moses in Exodus,

I myself will go with you, and I will give you victory"
(Exodus 33:14).

I'd like to end this chapter with the lyrics of the song that was written about John Henry. As you read, please envision yourself fighting the good fight of faith with God by your side. And the attitude of never giving up for what or Who we believe in. Let us be "Christ Driving" People.

John Henry was a little baby, sitting on his papa's knee. He picked up a hammer and a little piece of steel. Said, "Hammer's gonna be the death of me, Lord, Lord. Hammer's "Gonna be the death of me."

The captain said to John Henry,
"Gonna bring that steam drill 'round.
Gonna bring that steam drill out on the job.
Gonna whop that steel on down, Lord, Lord.
Gonna whop that steel on down."

John Henry told his captain,
"A man ain't nothing but a man.
But before I let your steam drill beat me down,
I'd die with a hammer in my hand, Lord, Lord.
I'd die with a hammer in my hand."

John Henry said to his shaker,
"Shaker, why don't you sing?
I'm throwin' thirty pounds from my hips on down.
Just listen to that cold steel ring, Lord, Lord.
Just listen to that cold steel ring."

John Henry said to his shaker,
"Shaker, you'd better pray.
'Cause if I miss that little piece of steel,
Tomorrow be your buryin' day, Lord, Lord.
Tomorrow be your buryin' day."

The shaker said to John Henry,
"I think this mountain's cavin' in!"
John Henry said to his shaker, "Man,
That ain't nothin' but my hammer suckin' wind! Lord, Lord.
That ain't nothin' but my hammer suckin' wind!"

Now the man that invented the steam drill,
Thought he was mighty fine.
But John Henry made fifteen feet,
The steam drill only made nine, Lord, Lord.
The steam drill only made nine.

John Henry hammered in the mountains,
His hammer was striking fire.
But he worked so hard, he broke his poor heart.
He laid down his hammer and he died, Lord, Lord.
He laid down his hammer and he died.

John Henry had a little woman,
Her name was Polly Ann.
John Henry took sick and went to his bed,
Polly Ann drove steel like a man, Lord, Lord.
Polly Ann drove steel like a man.

John Henry had a little baby,
You could hold him in the palm of your hand.
The last words I heard that poor boy say,
"My daddy was a steel-driving man, Lord, Lord.
My daddy was a steel-driving man."

They took John Henry to the graveyard,
And they buried him in the sand.
And every locomotive comes a-roaring by,

*Says "There lies a steel-driving man, Lord, Lord.
There lies a steel-driving man."*

*Well, every Monday morning,
When the bluebirds begin to sing.
You can hear John Henry a mile or more,
You can hear John Henry's hammer ring, Lord, Lord.
You can hear John Henry's hammer ring.*

JOY BUILDER TIP:
If you haven't already find a good Bible Study group or start one yourself. Online or in person or both

CHAPTER 6
A JOYFUL MIND

Finally, brothers and sisters, whatever is true, whatever is noble, whatever is right, whatever is pure, whatever is lovely, whatever is admirable—if anything is excellent or praiseworthy—think about such things. Whatever you have learned or received or heard from me, or seen in me—put it into practice. And the God of peace will be with you. (Philippians 4:8-9)

> It is nearly impossible to have a joyful life with a negative mind

It is nearly impossible to have a joyful life with a negative mind. What we think, we feel. What we feel, we do. What we do, we become. Okay, so it's not always that straightforward. I am not by any means saying that if you keep thinking about having a brand-new Ferrari, that one will show up on your doorstep the next day. But I am definitely saying that what we think about is one of the most important aspects of our lives. As Proverbs 23:7 states,

"For as he thinketh in his heart, so is he."

In other words, for the most part, we become what we think about most. And more importantly, how we think about God.

As A.W. Tozer once said,

"What comes into our minds when we think about God is the most important thing about us."

If our thoughts about God portray Him as some cruel taskmaster just waiting for the next time, He can pounce on us with judgment, then we will live our lives as such. But if we think He is the all-loving, all-knowing, omnipotent Father who loves us with an everlasting love, then we will also live accordingly.

> "What comes into our minds when we think about God is the most important thing about us."

The renewing of the mind to the Word of God Is one of the toughest tasks we, as Christians, will endeavor. However, the reward of it is eternally significant. Not just later on, but right here and right now. Like Hebrews 12:11 says,

"No discipline seems pleasant at the time, but painful. Later on, however, it produces a harvest of righteousness and peace for those who have been trained by it."

Renewing the mind is also one of the most important spiritual disciplines we will ever practice.

It Is easier said than done. But when we think joyful thoughts, we feel joyful feelings. Also, when we think negative thoughts, we will have negative feelings. But the practice of renewing the mind will only be beneficial with the Holy Spirit's help. I mean, He is the main Author of the Word. Who better to learn about a book than from the Author Himself?

It's so important to know that we can't always control what comes into our minds. But with the Spirit's help, we do have control of what "stays" in our minds. I think Martin Luther said it best in a quote I use quite often.

> It's so important to know that we can't always control what comes into our minds. But with the Spirit's help, we do have control of what "stays" in our minds.

"We can't keep the birds from flying over our heads, but we can keep them from building a nest in our hair" or if you are bald like me, in our heads.

It Is also very important to know that although the devil can send thoughts to us, he cannot read our minds. He is in no way omniscient like our good Father. But he is a master at studying our actions and behaviors. I hate to admit it, but if you are anything like me, sometimes all it takes is for the devil to send one negative thought. And then we take it from there and spin our own web of destruction. So, the best way to rid ourselves of the lies of the enemy is as soon as a negative thought or lie comes to your mind, go to The Word. If it doesn't line up with God's Word, then reject that thought right away and like Jesus in the wilderness, quote Scripture to replace it.

It Is so helpful to have a Bible Concordance. Because I have read many books about this method I am speaking of. Mainly from the Bible. But it was never spoken of how hard it is to jump on and find the right Scripture that combats your thoughts. That is why it is so important to have study tools. Like Strong's Concordance. Or topical references. So that way, if you are dealing with maybe thoughts of discouragement. Find the word courage and all the Scripture that speaks of it. I understand we can't always do this as we have our jobs and obligations. But I would definitely recommend making this a priority. You could get some 3×5 index cards with Scripture that deal with the negative thoughts you have currently been thinking or on your drive to work, listen to a great sermon or the audio Bible. Or get something like the YouVersion Bible app. There are so many ways in today's world that we can get the Word inside of us. But the main thing is, however, we go about it, that we do get The Word inside of us. So then faith cometh by hearing, and hearing by the word of God. (Romans 10:17)

In the Old Testament, the Hebrew word "hâgâh" is translated as "meditate." I found a great definition from a Google search. In the Bible, meditating on scripture means quietly reciting the words of scripture aloud or in your mind as a way to focus your attention so that these words become part of you.

For most people, the word meditate conjures up the thoughts of a Buddhist humming with their legs crossed to become one with self. It is sad to me as that form of eastern meditation is more dominant than true Biblical meditation. Eastern meditation teaches you to empty yourself. But Biblical meditation tells you to fill yourself with The Word. Not just positive affirmations but far greater the living Word of God. And we don't do it to be one with self but rather one with God.

> Biblical meditation tells you to fill yourself with The Word.

Sadly, by emptying yourself as most eastern meditation teaches, it can become very dangerous as you open yourself up to possible demonic influences. But when we fill ourselves with the Word by the only true form of meditation. We will not only think better and godly thoughts, but we will live better and godly lives. The goal is not to just mindlessly recite Scripture but to chew on it like a cow and its cud. It's kind of gross. But when a cow is eating its cud. It chews on it, spits it out, and chews on it again to make sure it gets every nutritional benefit out of the cud. So likewise, we want to do so with our Spiritual "Food". We want to speak, utter, and contemplate the Word so much that it becomes locked down in our hearts and flows out through our lives!

> *"I have hidden your word in my heart that I might not sin against you. Praise be to you, LORD; teach me your decrees. With my lips, I recount all the laws that come from your mouth."*
> **(Psalm 119:11-12)**

JOY BUILDER TIP

Either on 3×5 index cards or on your phone. Write out all the virtues in Phillipians 4:8 Finally, brothers and sisters, whatever is true, whatever is noble, whatever is right, whatever is pure, whatever is lovely, whatever is admirable—if anything is excellent or praiseworthy—think about such things. And write something in your life that correlates with each virtue. When you are feeling down or any day in general pull them out to remind to think on these things. And then think on them!

CHAPTER 7
TODAY IS THE DAY

Do not boast about tomorrow, for you do not know what a day may bring forth.
Proverbs 27:1.

"This is the day which the LORD hath made; we will rejoice and be glad in it."
Psalms 118:24.

In the hustle and bustle of everyday life, it's easy to get caught up in the routine and forget to truly embrace each day as a gift. We often find ourselves going through the motions without stopping to appreciate the beauty and wonder that surrounds us. However, life is too short to be lived this way. We are called to seize the day, to live with purpose and intention, making the most of every opportunity that comes our way.

> We are called to seize the day, to live with purpose and intention, making the most of every opportunity that comes our way.

One of the key principles of seizing the day is found in Ephesians 5:15-16, which says,

"Be very careful, then, how you live—not as unwise but as wise, making the most of every opportunity, because the days are evil."

This verse reminds us of the importance of being intentional with our time, making wise choices that align with our values and goals.

Living with purpose means being proactive rather than reactive, taking control of our lives, and making decisions that lead to fulfillment and happiness. It means being present in the moment, fully engaging with our surroundings and the people around us. It means pursuing our passions and dreams without letting fear or doubt hold us back.

Seizing the day also requires us to let go of the past and not worry excessively about the future. We cannot change what has already happened, and we cannot control what is yet to come. All we can do is focus on the present moment and make the most of the opportunities that are before us.

> When we live with purpose,
> we inspire others to do the same.

When we live with purpose, we inspire others to do the same. Our lives become a testament to the power of seizing the day, showing others that it is possible to live a life filled with meaning and significance. So let us embrace each day with gratitude and enthusiasm, seizing every opportunity that comes our way, and living life to the fullest.

Brothers and sisters, I do not consider that I have made it my own yet; but one thing I do: forgetting what lies behind and reaching forward to what lies ahead, I press on toward the goal to win the [heavenly] prize of the upward call of God in Christ Jesus. - Phillipians 3:13-14.

So if there is someone today that needs to be forgiven or told they are loved with all their imperfections, and how grateful you are for all they do and who they are, please do it today because tomorrow may never come! God be with you and seize this day!

"I call Heaven and Earth to witness against you today: I place before you Life and Death, Blessing and Curse. Choose life so that you and your children will live." - Deuteronomy 30:19-20.

I'd like to close this chapter with a quote from Frederick Buechner. He writes,

"Intellectually we all know that we will die, but we do not really know it in the sense that the knowledge becomes a part of us. We do not really know it in the sense of living as though it were true. On the contrary, we tend to live as though our lives would go on forever." Please seize the day!

JOY BUILDER TIP:
Instead of texting make a phone call with someone you confide and just have a genuine talk of what's on your heart and what God is doing in your life and then listen well when they speak

CHAPTER 8
THE RACE FOR JOY

Therefore I run in such a way, as not without aim; I box in such a way, as not beating the air; but I discipline my body and make it my slave, so that, after I have preached to others, I myself will not be disqualified.
1 Corinthians 9:26-27

In the city of Corinth, during the first century A.D., the apostle Paul wrote a letter to the Corinthians, urging them to live a life of purpose and dedication to their faith. In this letter, Paul used the metaphor of a race to describe the Christian life, saying,

"Do you not know that in a race all the runners run, but only one gets the prize? Run in such a way as to get the prize."

For many, this metaphor still resonates today. Life is often likened to a race—a journey filled with challenges, triumphs, and the need for endurance. Just as in a race, where runners must train, persevere, and stay focused on the finish line, so too must we navigate life with determination and purpose.

The race of life is not about competing against others but rather about striving to be the best version of oneself in Christ. It is about setting goals, overcoming obstacles, and staying true to one's values and beliefs. Just as a runner must push through fatigue and doubt to reach the finish line, so too must individuals push through life's challenges to achieve their goals and dreams.

> The race of life is not about competing against others but rather about striving to be the best version of oneself in Christ.

But the race of life is not just about personal achievement; it is also about the impact we have on others. Just as a runner can inspire and motivate those watching from the sidelines, so too can individuals inspire and motivate others through their words and actions. Each person's race is unique, but the goal remains the same—to live a life of purpose, dedication, and faith. When we have a purpose in life, it fills us with joy, and we look forward to waking up in the morning and seizing the day. But when we don't as the Word says

Where there is no vision, the people perish: but he that keepeth the law, happy is he. 19 A servant will not be corrected by words: for though he understands, he will not answer. Proverbs 29:18-19.

> "The difference between the impossible and the possible lies in determination"

I googled some inspirational quotes from famous track stars, and they really hit home. Here are a few of them. The only real limitation is the one you set for yourself. "

"The more you dream, the farther you get,"

"If you want to succeed, you have to let failure be your best friend!"

"Train hard, turn up, run your best, and the rest will take care of itself,"

"I don't think limits"

"Kill them with success and bury them with a smile,"

"The difference between the impossible and the possible lies in determination"

"To be number one, you have to train like you're number two."

"If I am still standing at the end of the race, hit me with a board and knock me down because that means I didn't run hard enough"

There is no greater race than the one we have in Christ.

Do you not know that in a race all the runners run [their very best to win], but only one receives the prize? Run [your race] in such a way that you may seize the prize and make it yours! 1 Corinthians 9:24.

JOY BUILDER TIP:

Use your memory to think of a special person and something they did for you. Try to really dig into the memory. Maybe what did it smell like then. Do you remember what time of year it was etc? Hold onto that memory as long as possible and thank God for that person and what they did for you

CHAPTER 9
CHOOSE JOY

I call Heaven and Earth to witness against you today: I place before you Life and Death, Blessing and Curse. Choose life so that you and your children will live. And love GOD, your God, listening obediently to him, firmly embracing him.
(Deuteronomy 30:19-20)

> When it really comes down to it, we only really have two choices in life: God or the devil, good or evil, right or wrong, left or right, life or death

Every time I think of making choices, I can't help but think of a friend of mine. In his more troubled days, at one of his stays in the county jail, he told me about another inmate who would always go around saying, "Everybody got choices." And how right he was. When you think about it, when it really comes down to it, we only really have two choices in life: God or the devil, good or evil, right or wrong, left or right, life or death. Every choice we make in life either brings life or brings death. It either adds to our lives or takes it away. As Jesus spoke of worry in Luke 12:25-26,

"Does worry add anything to your life? Can it add one more year, or even one day? So if worrying adds nothing but actually subtracts from your life, why would you worry about God's care of you?

> Every choice we make in life either brings life or brings death.

Just like we choose to worry, we must also choose to be joyful. Of course, that is easier said than done. But with God, all things are possible. We must be very intentional about what we put in our minds and how we talk to ourselves. One of the best quotes I have heard on this matter is from the great late Dr. Martyn Lloyd Jones: "Have you realized that most of your unhappiness in life is due to the fact that you are listening to yourself instead of talking to yourself? Take those thoughts that come to you the moment you wake up in the morning. You have not originated them, but they are talking to you. They bring back the problems of yesterday, etc. Somebody is talking. Who is talking to you? Your self is talking to you. Now, this man's treatment [in Psalm 42] was this: instead of allowing this self to talk to him, he starts talking to himself. 'Why art thou cast down, O my soul?' he asks. His soul had been depressing him, crushing him. So he stands up and says, 'Self, listen for a moment, I will speak to you.'"

> In order for change to happen, we have to make changes and choices

In order for change to happen, we have to make changes and choices. It's time we take back the territory the enemy has stolen by "stirring ourselves up in the Lord!" For this reason, I remind you to stir into flame the gift of God that you have through the imposition of my hands.

For God did not give us a spirit of cowardice but rather of power and love and self-control
(2 Timothy 1:6-7).

> Whatever is true, whatever is noble, whatever is right, whatever is pure, whatever is lovely, whatever is admirable—if anything is excellent or praiseworthy. Think on these things

Take a second with yourself and think about what you are thinking about. Are they thoughts of hate, envy, worry, negativity, or depression? You can even be depressed about being depressed. Or are your thoughts of whatever is true, whatever is noble, whatever is right, whatever is pure, whatever is lovely, whatever is admirable—if anything is excellent or praiseworthy. Think on these things (Philippians 4:8-9).

The great news is that if your thoughts are not aligned with the latter things, they can be! But we must choose to think on them. They certainly will not always come naturally. That is until we make a habit of them.

It's very easy, especially today, to focus on the negative. And the positive seems so far out of reach sometimes. But with the Holy Spirit's help and the Word of God, we can truly live out the promise in Romans 12:2:

"Do not conform to the pattern of this world, but be transformed by the renewing of your mind. Then you will be able to test and approve what God's will is—his good, pleasing, and perfect will."

I remind you again of the verse at the beginning of this chapter, where God sets before us life and death. And He beckons us to choose life so that we might live and live in the abundant joy of Jesus no matter what comes our way. "Everybody got choices." Please choose Jesus, and joy will follow.

JOY BUILDER TIP:

Think of a dream or a way you can serve that God put on your heart. If possible take one step today aiming towards that dream. Even just thinking about that dream will bring joy. But acting on it of course with God's help will bring so much more!

CHAPTER 10
BIBLICAL JOY

Delight yourself in the LORD, and He will give you the desires of your heart".
Psalm 37:4

Joy is the fruit of a right relation with God. It is not something people can create by their own efforts. The Bible distinguishes joy from pleasure. The Greek word for pleasure is the word from which we get our word "hedonism the philosophy of "self-centered pleasure seeking. Paul referred to false teachers as

> Joy is the fruit of a right relation with God. It is not something people can create by their own efforts.

"lovers of pleasure rather than lovers of God"
(2 Tim. 3:4 HCSB).

The Bible warns that self-indulgent pleasure seeking does not lead to happiness and fulfill- ment. Ecclesiastes 2:1-11 records the sad testi- mony of one who sought to build his life on pleasure seeking. The search left him empty and disillusioned. Proverbs 14:13 offers insight into this way of life,

"Even in laughter a heart may be sad"
(HCSB).

Cares, riches, and pleasures rob people of the possibility of fruitful living (Luke 8:14). Pleasure seeking often enslaves people in a vicious cycle of addiction (Titus 3:3). The self- indulgent person, according to 1 Tim. 5:6 is dead while seeming still to be alive.

> Many people think that God is the great killjoy. Nothing could be a bigger lie. God Him- self knows joy, and He wants His people to know joy

Many people think that God is the great killjoy. Nothing could be a bigger lie. God Him- self knows joy, and He wants His people to know joy. Psalm 104:31 speaks of God Himself rejoic- ing in His creative works. Isaiah 65:18 speaks of God rejoicing over His redeemed people who will be to Him "a joy"

(Holmans illustrated Bible Dictionary Joy) You won't hear this from many in the pulpit, but sin "can" be fun. Otherwise, we wouldn't do it. But as all of us know, that fun is only for a season and sometimes can even lead to death. But the crazy part is that even though we have that knowledge, it definitely doesn't always stop us from doing it. But rather than try to sin less, we need to replace it with something or rather Someone that brings greater "joy" than any sin could ever bring, and it's not temporal. Just telling our brothers and sisters to stop sinning without leading them in the way of the Spirit is like telling a 2 year old to stop crying without comforting them. Rather I say then:

> *Walk in the Spirit, and you shall not fulfill the lust of the flesh. For the flesh lusts against the Spirit, and the Spirit against the flesh; and these are contrary to one another, so that you do not do the things that you wish. But if you are led by the Spirit, you are not under the law.*
> **Galatians 5:16-18.**

Notice it does not say don't fulfill the lusts of the flesh and instead walk in the Spirit. It says walk in The Spirit "so you don't " fulfill the lusts of the flesh. I like what Pastor Tony Evans says about just trying to sin less without walking in the Spirit. He calls it "sin management." I hate to break to you, left to our own devices we can never manage sin. But even better, we can overcome it!

Do not be overcome by evil, but overcome evil with good Romans 12:21.

> Sin wants you to itself. When we are honed in on the sin that cripples us most, we seem to forget that there is a whole world of possibilities and pleasure out there for us to find.

Sin wants you to itself. When we are honed in on the sin that cripples us most, we seem to forget that there is a whole world of possibilities and pleasure out there for us to find. Of course, all in Christ. But sin takes no prisoners. It doesn't care about you, and it never will. It doesn't care whether you are black or white, woman or man or rich or poor. It seeks only to please its father, the devil. Of course, as I speak, sin is not a person. But it is the ultimate disease that plagues our souls and keeps us away from the Joy In Jesus. It thrives best in the darkness. There is only one way to expose it and be rid of it.

The light shines in the darkness, and the darkness has not overcome it. John 1:5.

It's the same story from the beginning of time.

The earth was without form and void, and darkness was over the face of the deep. And the Spirit of God was hovering over the face of the waters. 3 And God said, "Let there be light," and there was light.

Genesis 1:2-3.

I believe God is saying that to us today when we are so entangled in the darkness of our sins. "Let there be light!". And not just any light. The only Light we will ever need. John 8:12 –

Once again, Jesus spoke to the people and said, "I am the light of the world. Whoever follows Me will never walk in the darkness, but will have the light of life.".

> No sin ever will ever give us the joy we so desperately yearn for.

And in Him, we are also lights to the world! You are the light of the world. A city on a hill can not be hidden. Matthew 5:14. Go let your light shine! No sin ever will ever give us the joy we so desperately yearn for. No matter how long or how many times we do it. Never not once in history will there ever be anything good that comes out of sin except when God takes it and makes good out of it! The closer we get to the Light, the more we will see this world and sin as it really is. But even greater, we can live with a joy unspeakable! That the world, the flesh, and the devil can never strip away from us!

JOY BUILDER TIP:

Tell as many people possible today that you love them and if they are special to you tell them why you love them

CHAPTER 11
MAN'S CHIEF END

"I will take joy in the God of my salvation".
Habakkuk 3:18:

The Westminster Shorter Catechism asks and answers this question:

"What is the chief end of man?" The answer is, "Man's chief end is to glorify God and to enjoy him forever."

I love Pastor John Piper's version of it. He says

"man's chief end is to glorify God "by" enjoying Him forever."

> It is one thing to know a lot "about" Jesus, but a whole other thing to "know" Jesus.

As we journey on our quest for the joy of Jesus, we will stumble on probably the most pivotal moment of all. We can even call it a plot twist. Here it is: The joy of Jesus for us is actually Jesus Himself! Boom. Curtain closes. Lights out. But not so fast. It is one thing to know a lot "about" Jesus, but a whole other thing to "know" Jesus. The Hebrew term for the word "know" is Yada, and it has a wider sweep than the English word "know." It includes perceiving, learning, understanding, willing, performing, and experiencing.

In Ancient Hebrew thought, the idea of "knowing" is similar to our understanding but is more personal and intimate. Actually, to express the thought even further, the word "know" in the

Bible a lot of times is interchangeable with sexual intimacy. Of course, not speaking morbidly. But as we know, sex is one of the most intimate things God created. Think about when you first met your partner. When you couldn't eat or sleep without thinking about them. You couldn't get their face out of your mind or name off of your tongue. Every moment you lived and breathed, you made it about them. Well, minus the sexual part, that is how we should feel about God, but even so much more!

For God is my record, how greatly I long after you all in the bowels of Jesus Christ. Phillipians 1:8.

As we most know, when we feel that intimate sensation, when we think or are around our partner, it is said that it comes from our bowels. The Greek word for "bowels" is splanchnon. Which can denote inward affection, "or "tender mercy." Not to be gross, but you know that feeling when you have to go to the bathroom really bad. But not the bad kind of experience. Forgive me, Lord and ladies, but men, you know when you start your morning with a good cup of coffee, maybe sitting on the toilet, hopefully reading some Christian literature. That's all I'm saying about that. But I think you get the point. As Jesus said,

love the Lord your God with all your heart and with all your soul and with all your mind.'
Matthew 22:37.

I am by no means changing Scripture, but our bowels could be included in that. Literally giving everything we have for the One who gave everything for us so that we might become like Him!

When most people think of eternal life, they think about life after death. Which, of course, is part of it. But that definition falls short. The Bible says:

"Now this is eternal life: that they know you, the only true God, and Jesus Christ, whom you have sent."
John 17:3.

And this life doesn't start after we die. It starts the moment we give our lives to Christ! I have heard a great and so true saying:

> *"He who is born once dies twice. But he who is born twice dies once."*

> Eternal Life doesn't start after we die. It starts the moment we give our lives to Christ!

There is no life outside of Christ. I don't say to offend. But if you aren't living for Him, who are you living for? It has well been said that one of the atheists' saddest moments is when he is beyond thankful for something but has no One to thank. So if we want that everlasting joy, we must make it our chief end to glorify God by enjoying Him forever. That is when life at its best starts to begin. There is no greater joy than knowing and being in the presence of our Creator.

> *"You make known to me the path of life; in your presence, there is fullness of joy; at your right hand are pleasures forevermore."*
> **Psalm 16:11.**

I want to end this chapter with an amazing quote from the "Prince of preachers" Charles Spurgeon:

"God has ordained it so that a spiritual man is wretched without the love of God in his heart. If you and I want present happiness without God, we had better be sinners outright and live upon this world than try to be happy in religion without communion with Jesus. Present happiness for a genuine Christian in the absence of Christ is an absolute impossibility. We must have God or we are of all men most miserable."

JOY BUILDER TIP:

Think of one hobby or something you've always wanted to do(approved by God) that you maybe never had time for or motivation to do so at that time. Take one step towards that hobby. I.e. buy your first guitar. Try writing your first poem. Get creative with it!

CHAPTER 12
A WANT THAT NEVER ENDS

The guilty undertaker sighs

The lonesome organ grinder cries

The silver saxophones say I should refuse you

The cracked bells and washed-out horns

> "We have as much of God as we actually want."

Blow into my face with scorn, but it's

Not that way, I wasn't born to lose you

I want you

I want you

I want you, so bad-Bob Dylan

A.W. Tozer is credited with saying,

"We have as much of God as we actually want."

God couldn't have shown us He wanted us more than by dying on the Cross so we could fellowship with Him again.

> *Greater love has no one than this: to lay down one's life for one's friends.*
> **John 15:13.**

> When we give our old selves away, we actually become our true selves.

So there is no question how much He wants us. But the question is how bad do we want Him. I should be very clear at the forefront that I am not suggesting a works based performance to show God how much we want Him. But rather the complete opposite. One of the best ways to demonstrate our want is to completely and fully surrender to Him in every area of our life. I can't help but be reminded of the once very popular U2 song. With or Without You. Specifically, the line that says "and you give yourself away." That is exactly what we do when we surrender to God. But the irony is that when we give our old selves away, we actually become our true selves. The Greek word for surrender is "Paradidōmi".

In the New Testament, paradidōmi appears about 120 times, and in the Greek Old Testament, it appears over 200 times. It can mean to give into the hands of another, to give over into one's power. It can also mean to deliver one to be taught or molded. I love that last definition. By surrendering to God, we are being taught and molded in the Way. Myself included sometimes surrender can be a scary word. A lot of times, we think when we surrender to God that He is going to take all the fun and joy out of our lives. But that couldn't be further from the truth! On the contrary, we don't even know what life is until we fully surrender to Him and His ways. That is when life begins at its best! Delight yourself also in the LORD, and He shall give you the desires of your heart." Psalm 37:4. It really comes down to a matter of trust. But He knows us far more than we know ourselves! Your Father knows what you need before you ask him. Matthew 6:8. We can never out give or out love or out anything compared to our Creator! That's why we can never get enough of Him. Yet at the same time, He is more than enough, and we can be completely satisfied in Him while we continue to seek Him! One thing have I asked of the Lord, that will I seek after: that I may dwell in the house of the Lord all the days of my life, to gaze upon the beauty of the Lord and to inquire in his temple" Psalm 27:4.

The young lions suffer want and hunger; but those who seek the Lord lack no good thing. " Psalm 34:10. We are all most likely familiar with the phrase "I want(something or someone) So bad I could die for it. If we but only had that same attitude towards our relationship with God, we would do great damage to the Kingdom! In a God way, of course. We all know the famous Psalm 23. The Lord is my Shepherd I shall not want. In this verse, the Psalmist is not speaking of our want for God. But rather, the things we need or want. I am by no means changing the Bible but expressing a point. "The Lord is our shepherd, and we "shall want Him" all the days of our lives. Because when we want God before anything in all creation, that is when true joy and fellowship begins and never ends. So like in the opening of this chapter let us apply The words of Bob Dylan to our Magnificent Creator. I want you, I want you, I want you so bad. And we will truly never be in want again!

JOY BUILDER TIP:

Write out a list of all the people in your life that you are grateful for. Spend time with God thanking Him for them and pray for them

CHAPTER 13
A DIFFERENT KIND OF JOY

> Jesus's joy was not the fleeting happiness that comes from worldly pleasures. It was a deep, abiding joy that stemmed from his unwavering faith and connection to God.

In the bustling streets of Jerusalem, amidst the ancient stones and bustling crowds, there was a man unlike any other. His name was Jesus, and wherever he went, he carried with him a joy that seemed to transcend the ordinary. His presence was a beacon of hope, and his words were like streams of living water, refreshing the souls of those who listened. Jesus's joy was not the fleeting happiness that comes from worldly pleasures. It was a deep, abiding joy that stemmed from his unwavering faith and connection to God. He knew the challenges and sorrows of life, yet his spirit remained unbroken, his joy unshakeable. I and the Father are one. John 10:30

One of the most striking aspects of Jesus's joy was its inclusivity. He welcomed everyone, regardless of their background or circumstances, and his joy knew no bounds. Whether he was dining with tax collectors and sinners or healing the sick and comforting the downtrodden, Jesus's joy was a constant presence, illuminating the lives of those around him.

In Jesus, people found not only a teacher and a healer but also a friend who shared in their joys and sorrows. His compassion knew no bounds, and his love was a light that pierced the darkness of despair.

> In Jesus, people found not only a teacher and a healer but also a friend who shared in their joys and sorrows.

Jesus's joy was also a source of strength. In the face of opposition and persecution, he remained steadfast, his joy serving as a shield against doubt and fear. He knew that the path he walked was not an easy one, yet he faced it with courage and conviction, knowing that his joy would sustain him.

Who for the joy that was set before him endured the cross, despising the shame, and is set down at the right hand of the throne of God."
Hebrews 12:2

For those who followed Jesus, his joy became a model to emulate. They, too, learned to find joy in serving others, in showing compassion and forgiveness, and in seeking God's will above all else. They discovered that true joy comes not from selfish pursuits but from selfless love and devotion to God.

*As Jesus Himself, how he said,
It is more blessed to give than to receive.*
Acts 20:35

Today, the joy of Jesus continues to shine brightly in the hearts of believers around the world. It is a joy that transcends time and space, a joy that offers hope in the midst of despair, and a joy that reminds us that no matter how dark the night may seem, the dawn of a new day is always near.

Do not be anxious about anything, but in every situation, by prayer and petition, with thanksgiving, present your requests to God. And the peace of God, which transcends all understanding, will guard your hearts and your minds in Christ Jesus. Phillipians 4:6-7 (NIV).

As we journey through life, may we be inspired by the joy of Jesus, and may we, too, become beacons of light, illuminating the world with love, compassion, and unwavering faith.

JOY BUILDER TIP:
Find and watch a good Biblical sermon on Joy. I recommend anything from Charles Stanley. Alistair Begg, Craig Groeschel, Tony Evans or someone from your local church.

CHAPTER 14
FIGHTING FOR JOY THROUGH FAITH

"We fight for joy. But we fight as those who are saved by grace and held by Christ. We say...that our night will soon- in God's good timing- turn to day. God is glorified in his people by the way we experience Him, not merely by the way we think about Him."
-John Piper

You make known to me the path of life; in your presence there is fullness of joy; at your right hand are pleasures forevermore"
-The Bible Psalm 16:11

> You make known to me the path of life; in your presence there is fullness of joy; at your right hand are pleasures forevermore"

As John Piper states it is merely not enough to just think about God. Although that is eternally important. However, I could think about taking a walk all day, but that doesn't mean I'm going to do it. As James states

"Faith without action is dead"

And in the words of the music group 311

"nothing good comes easily sometimes you've got to fight".

There are not many more things the devil loves than a Christian without joy. This is just a personal thought. But I believe the devil doesn't even care so much that we love God. But he does care when we love God first and above all else. I don't believe the devil has any love in him. But he "loves" when the object of our affection is a close friend or family member. Of course we are supposed to love them. But as Jesus said himself.

> *"If anyone comes to me and does not hate his own father and mother, wife and children, brothers and sisters—yes, and even his own life—he cannot be my disciple.*
> **Luke 14:26.**

Sadly this is often a very misused and misquoted Scripture. Now I know my fundamentalist friends may disagree. And I love them. But they are not disagreeing with me but The Word. Because when Jesus uses the word hate, the original Greek actually says "to prefer more than". As Jesus would never teach us to hate anyone in the literal sense. But I'm sure many have had a hay day with this Scripture. All of this is to say if we prefer or choose anything above our Creator. Our worship becomes dangerous and breeds idolatry. I've heard it well said of Satan's "LSD" Lust Sin and Death. Worship is a matter of the heart.

(Worship is a matter of the heart)

Above all else, guard your heart, for It is the wellspring of life"
(Proverbs 4:23).

As the 90s song goes "love hurts" and it truly does at times.

But love also bears all things [regardless of what comes], believes all things [looking for the best in each one], hopes all things [remaining steadfast during difficult times], endures all things [without weakening]. Love never fails [it never fades nor ends]. 1 Corinthians 13:6-8.

In fact we wouldn't even know true love if we didn't know God. Because God is love. And He loved us way before we loved Him.

1 John 4:8 and 19.

But I assure you that thing or person that you may have loved above God. Will always in some way let you down. But I believe it is good sometimes to be let down by people or things as it forces you to look up to the One who will never let you down. When you worship and put God first in all things.

All things will work together for good. For those who love Him and are called according to His purpose. Romans 8:28

> Put God first and you'll never be last!

So I beseech you with all that is in me. Put God first and you'll never be last! Worship the Creator over the creature and watch the amazing things He will do through you and to you! But most of all worship Him because He is God and we are not. I pray with all my heart that our worship will never be distorted again! I'd like to end this chapter with a quote from the prince of preachers Charles Spurgeon

"If God were material, it might be right to worship him with material substances; if God were like to ourselves, it might be well for us to give a sacrifice congenial to humanity; but being as he is, pure spirit, he must be worshipped in spirit. "Also the words of Jesus in Matthew 22:37

Love the Lord your God with all your heart and with all your soul and with all your mind.

JOY BUILDER TIP:

This tip definitely depends on how certain people are. But try to hug as many people possible today. If you have no one to hug or are alone for the day. Hug yourself. I don't say this next part as mystical in biblical notion. But every time you hug imagine that you are hugging Jesus.

CHAPTER 15
JOY IN THE MIDST OF SUFFERING

My brethren, count it all joy when ye fall into divers temptations;

Knowing this, that the trying of your faith worketh patience.

But let patience have her perfect work, that ye may be perfect and entire, wanting nothing.

If any of you lack wisdom, let him ask of God, that giveth to all men liberally, and upbraideth not; and it shall be given him.

But let him ask in faith, nothing wavering. For he that wavereth is like a wave of the sea driven with the wind and tossed.
James 1:2-6

> We would never know or appreciate joy if we never faced suffering.

At first sight you might think James sounds crazy. Joy while you are suffering? It is very important to know however, that James is not saying be joyful "for" the trials themselves but rather be joyful knowing that "through" the trial God is working something good out inside of us. I don't care how you look at it, suffering is never fun. But if we are being honest most of us would admit that it's in these moments that we truly grow closer to God. And although we would never want to go back to them, we can look back now with full gratitude that we went through it. In fact we would never know or appreciate joy if we never faced suffering. Notice in the infamous Psalm 23. That David says "though I walk "through" the valley of the shadow of death" (emphasis added). He didn't say above or go around or even take it away. He said through. But goes on to say "I will fear no evil for God is with me". And God is with you too brave warrior. Whether a believer or not we all suffer, but the eternal difference is that as a believer we go through suffering with the Creator of the universe on our side and we are never alone. As you go throughout your week, I beseech you to meditate on this and repeat it over and over until it is locked deep down in your heart." I will fear no evil for God is with me". No matter what you face, remind yourself of this promise and through Him you can truly overcome anything that comes your way.

> *Little children, you are from God and have overcome them, for he who is in you is greater than he who is in the world.*
> ***1 John 4:4***

That is why we can have joy in suffering. Because we know that God is always with us and He gives nothing but His best. For His glory and our good.

Weeping may endure for the night. But joy cometh in the morning Psalm 30:5

(Dark days don't last forever. But God's joy and love do)

I've heard it said that dark days don't last forever. But God's joy and love do. As James says

Yet you do not know [the least thing] about what may happen in your life tomorrow. [What is secure in your life?] You are *merely* a vapor [like a puff of smoke or a wisp of steam from a cooking pot] that is visible for a little while and then vanishes [into thin air].

James 4:14.

We really do have such a short time down here. Hasn't the devil stolen enough from you and the ones you love?? He knows his time is short. He also knows that he can never steal our salvation or separate us from Christ. But he will do everything possible to make us miserable on our journey till we get to heaven. One of the biggest black eyes we can ever give him is living out the joy of the Lord all the days of our lives. As I close out this chapter I am reminded of a great quote from the Prince of preachers himself Charles Spurgeon

"It Is for love; in the gospel, sinner, you are invited to be reconciled to God, you are assured that God forgives your sins, ceases to be angry, and would have you reconciled to him through his Son. Thus love is established between God and the soul. Then it is for laughter, for happiness, for joy. Those who come to God in Christ Jesus, and believe in him, have their hearts filled with overflowing peace, which calm lake of peace often lifts up itself in waves of joy, which clap their hands in exultation. It is not to sorrow but to joy that the great King invites his subjects, when he glorifies his Son Jesus. It is not that you may be distressed, but that you may be delighted that he bids you believe in the crucified Savior and live."

Believe and live he says! We have the greatest Joy that no one can take from us! Don't let the devil steal one more moment from you. He is on a short leash and soon His time will be no more. But we are also on a short walk but through Christ we will live forever. So in the midst of suffering remember that great truth. Not just when that day comes but let it lift up your soul in this very moment! And say like King David. I will fear no evil for God is with me. He is with you as well brave soul. Please don't ever forget that ultimate truth. You got this!

JOY BUILDER TIP:

Most of us already know this. But I want us to know it so much so that it becomes locked in our heart and spills out to everyone we encounter. Throughout the day say to yourself "God loves me" if possible, say it out loud. Say it until you feel and know it with full conviction

CHAPTER 16
FINDING JOY IN THE WORD OF GOD

*I have hidden your word in my heart that
I might not sin against you.*
Psalm 119:11

The Bible is often called the "Living Word" because it speaks to us at every stage of life. Its verses have the power to penetrate the deepest recesses of our hearts, offering hope, guidance, correction, and, perhaps most overlooked, joy. But in a world filled with distractions, how do we rediscover this joy? How do we engage with the Scriptures in a way that reignites our passion and fills us with divine happiness? This chapter will explore the beauty and fulfillment that comes from immersing ourselves in the Word of God.

> The Word of God is more than just a collection of historical writings, poetry, and prophecy. It is a divine revelation given to humanity

THE SOURCE OF ETERNAL JOY

The Word of God is more than just a collection of historical writings, poetry, and prophecy. It is a divine revelation given to humanity, filled with God's wisdom, promises, and plan for redemption. In its pages, we find the very essence of joy because the Bible reveals who God is. And in knowing God, we find joy.

Psalm 16:11 tells us,

"You make known to me the path of life; in your presence there is fullness of joy; at your right hand are pleasures forevermore."

This verse reflects the heart of biblical joy—it is found in God's presence. Every time we open the Bible, we step into the presence of God, where joy abounds. When we understand that the Bible is a love letter from the Creator, the natural response is to delight in it.

But the truth is, not everyone feels joy when reading the Bible. For some, it might feel like a duty or a task to check off a list. Yet, the Bible was never meant to be a mere religious obligation. It was given to be a wellspring of life, a source of deep and abiding joy that sustains us.

JOY COMES FROM UNDERSTANDING

> "The joy of the Lord is your strength."

Nehemiah 8:10 famously states,

"The joy of the Lord is your strength."

What's fascinating about this verse is the context in which it was written. The people of Israel had just heard the Law read aloud to them, many for the first time in their lives. Their initial reaction was one of grief and sorrow because they realized how far they had strayed from God's commandments. But Nehemiah encouraged them, telling them that their newfound understanding should not lead to sorrow but to joy. Why? Because understanding the Word of God brings us closer to God, and that closeness births joy.

When we truly understand the Scriptures—when we see the love of God revealed in every command, the mercy shown in every story, the redemption promised in every prophecy—our hearts are filled with joy. We realize that the Word of God is not there to condemn us but to guide us into a life of fulfillment and peace. It is in this understanding that we find true joy.

JOY IN GOD'S PROMISES

One of the richest sources of joy in the Word of God is found in His promises. The Bible is filled with promises that speak to every aspect of our lives—promises of provision, protection, peace, and, most importantly, salvation. When we meditate on these promises, we are reminded that God is faithful, and that brings us joy.

> When we meditate on these promises, we are reminded that God is faithful, and that brings us joy. For example, consider the promise found in Romans 8:28:

"And we know that in all things God works for the good of those who love him, who have been called according to his purpose."

This is not just a hopeful thought; it's a guaranteed promise from God. When life feels uncertain, overwhelming, or chaotic, this verse brings reassurance, and with it, joy. We know that no matter what happens, God is working all things for our good.

Another powerful promise is found in Isaiah 40:31: "But those who hope in the Lord will renew their strength. They will soar on wings like eagles; they will run and not grow weary, they will walk and not be faint." This verse speaks to the weariness we often feel in life, but it also gives us hope and joy because we know that God is our strength. Meditating on promises like these strengthens our faith and fills our hearts with joy.

JOY IN THE DISCIPLINE OF THE WORD

> The Bible encourages us to meditate on God's Word day and night

Joy is not always immediate. Sometimes, we find it through persistence and discipline. The Bible encourages us to meditate on God's Word day and night (Joshua 1:8), not just when it feels convenient or when we're in the mood. At times, joy comes after we've wrestled with difficult passages, waited patiently in prayer, or walked through seasons of spiritual dryness.

Hebrews 12:11 tells us,

"No discipline seems pleasant at the time, but painful. Later on, however, it produces a harvest of righteousness and peace for those who have been trained by it."

This is also true of the discipline of reading and studying the Word of God. In seasons when it feels like a struggle, the joy may not be immediate, but it will come. God rewards those who diligently seek Him, and one of those rewards is joy.

JOY IN SHARING THE WORD

One of the greatest joys we experience as believers is sharing the Word of God with others. When we testify to what God has done in our lives or when we lead someone to a deeper understanding of Scripture, our joy is multiplied. The apostle John wrote in 3 John 1:4,

"I have no greater joy than to hear that my children are walking in the truth."

There is a profound joy that comes when we see others embrace the truth of God's Word and grow in their faith.

Whether it's through teaching, encouraging a friend with a verse, or living out the principles of Scripture, sharing the Word allows us to participate in God's work, and that is deeply satisfying. We become part of the unfolding story of redemption, and that fills us with a joy that goes beyond ourselves.

JOY AS A FRUIT OF THE WORD

> The more we immerse ourselves in Scripture, the more the Holy Spirit transforms us.

Finally, joy is a fruit of the Spirit (Galatians 5:22), and the Spirit works through the Word of God. The more we immerse ourselves in Scripture, the more the Holy Spirit transforms us. As we read, meditate, and apply the Word, the fruit of joy begins to flourish in our lives. This joy is not dependent on our circumstances, but on the unchanging nature of God and His eternal Word.

In conclusion, finding joy in the Word of God is not a fleeting experience but a lifelong journey. It is a joy that grows as we grow in our understanding, our trust in God's promises, and our commitment to His truth. The Bible is not just a book; it is a pathway to divine joy—a joy that sustains us in all seasons of life. As we continue to seek God through His Word, may we always discover the deep and lasting joy that only He can provide.

JOY BUILDER TIP:

If you don't already have one find a prayer partner or two. Depending on your schedule try to connect once a week and pray your hearts out together! Remember Ecclesiastes 4:12 And if a man prevail against him that is alone, two shall withstand him; and a threefold cord is not quickly broken.

CHAPTER 17

FINDING JOY IN THE HOLY SPIRIT

For the kingdom of God is not a matter of eating and drinking, but of righteousness, peace and joy in the Holy Spirit, because anyone who serves Christ in this way is pleasing to God and receives human approval".
Romans 4:17-18

In the journey of faith, one of the greatest gifts God has given us is His Holy Spirit. Jesus promised,

"I will ask the Father, and he will give you another advocate to help you and be with you forever—the Spirit of truth"
(John 14:16-17).

The Holy Spirit, who dwells within every believer, is a source of power, guidance, and, perhaps most profoundly, joy. Yet, many Christians live unaware of the deep joy that the Holy Spirit offers. How can we experience this joy in our daily lives, and what does it look like to live with the fullness of the Holy Spirit's joy?

This chapter explores how the Holy Spirit is the wellspring of joy for every believer and how we can learn to experience this joy in every season of life.

THE HOLY SPIRIT AND JOY: A DIVINE CONNECTION

The Bible makes it clear that joy is a direct product of the Holy Spirit's presence in our lives. Galatians 5:22 lists joy as one of the fruits of the Spirit, meaning that when the Spirit Is actively working in and through us, joy naturally follows. This is not a superficial or temporary happiness but a deep, abiding joy that transcends circumstances.

> The Bible makes it clear that joy is a direct product of the Holy Spirit's presence in our lives.

Romans 14:17 reminds us,

"For the kingdom of God is not a matter of eating and drinking, but of righteousness, peace, and joy in the Holy Spirit."

Joy is part of the very essence of life in the Spirit. It is not something we manufacture on our own or experience only during times of ease; it is a joy that the Holy Spirit places deep within us, rooted in God's presence and His eternal promises.

The connection between the Holy Spirit and joy is crucial. True joy cannot be found apart from Him. While the world often searches for happiness in external pleasures and circumstances, the Holy Spirit provides joy that is not dependent on the shifting tides of life. This joy is a result of being filled with the presence of God Himself.

JOY IN THE PRESENCE OF THE SPIRIT

In the presence of the Holy Spirit, we experience the fullness of joy. Psalm 16:11 beautifully declares,

"You make known to me the path of life; in your presence there is fullness of joy; at your right hand are pleasures forevermore."

The Holy Spirit, as the third person of the Trinity, brings us into the very presence of God. The joy we experience is a result of this intimate relationship with the living God.

> The joy we experience is a result of this intimate relationship with the living God.

This is why believers can experience joy even in difficult circumstances. The apostle Paul, while imprisoned, wrote to the Philippians,

"Rejoice in the Lord always. I will say it again: Rejoice!"
(Philippians 4:4).

How could Paul express joy in such a dire situation? The answer lies in his relationship with the Holy Spirit. His joy was not dependent on his surroundings but on the Spirit of God who lived within him.

The same is true for us. The Holy Spirit enables us to have joy even when life is hard. When we face trials, hardships, or uncertainty, the Spirit remains our constant source of joy. He reminds us of God's faithfulness, His unchanging nature, and His eternal promises. In the darkest moments, the Holy Spirit whispers to our hearts, reassuring us of God's love and purpose, filling us with a supernatural joy that defies logic.

THE SPIRIT'S ROLE IN LEADING US TO JOY

One of the most powerful ways the Holy Spirit leads us to joy is by guiding us into the truth of God's Word and into deeper relationship with Jesus Christ. In John 16:13-14, Jesus explains,

"But when he, the Spirit of truth, comes, he will guide you into all the truth... He will glorify me because it is from me that he will receive what he will make known to you."

The Holy Spirit Is constantly pointing us back to Jesus, the source of all joy. He reveals to us the beauty of Christ's character,

His work on the cross, and the hope of His return. As the Spirit deepens our understanding of who Jesus is and what He has done for us, our hearts are filled with joy.

> The Holy Spirit Is constantly pointing us back to Jesus, the source of all joy.

Consider the moment of salvation. When the Holy Spirit opens our eyes to the truth of the gospel and we place our faith in Jesus, the result is an overwhelming joy. We experience the joy of forgiveness, the joy of reconciliation with God, and the joy of new life in Christ. This initial joy is not meant to be a one-time experience; the Holy Spirit continues to deepen and renew our joy as we grow in our relationship with Jesus.

JOY IN THE SPIRIT'S POWER

The Holy Spirit also empowers us for Christian living, and with that power comes joy. In Acts 1:8, Jesus promised His disciples,

"You will receive power when the Holy Spirit comes on you."

This power is not just for boldness in ministry but also for living out the Christian life in joy.

When we rely on the Holy Spirit, we are strengthened to overcome challenges, resist temptation, and endure hardship. This empowerment brings joy because we are no longer trying to live the Christian life in our own strength. Instead, we are living by the power of God Himself. There is joy in knowing that the same Spirit who raised Christ from the dead is at work within us (Romans 8:11), enabling us to live in victory.

> When we rely on the Holy Spirit, we are strengthened to overcome challenges, resist temptation, and endure hardship.

This joy in the Spirit's power is evident in the early church. Acts 13:52 describes the disciples as *"filled with joy and with the Holy Spirit."*

Despite facing persecution and opposition, the disciples were overflowing with joy because they were filled with the Spirit. Their joy was not dependent on favorable circumstances but on the indwelling presence of the Holy Spirit, who empowered them to face adversity with confidence and peace.

THE SPIRIT'S JOY IN FELLOWSHIP AND UNITY

Another beautiful aspect of the Holy Spirit's work is how He fosters joy in the community of believers. The Spirit unites us with other Christians, and in that unity, we find joy. Fellowship with other believers, worship, and communal prayer are moments where the joy of the Holy Spirit is tangibly felt.

Consider how often in the book of Acts we see believers gathering together, praying, worshiping, and sharing meals. In these moments of Spirit-led community, there was great joy. Acts 2:46-47 tells us,

"They broke bread in their homes and ate together with glad and sincere hearts, praising God and enjoying the favor of all the people."

> This joy that comes from fellowship with others is not merely social happiness; it is the joy that arises when believers are united by the Holy Spirit.

This joy that comes from fellowship with others is not merely social happiness; it is the joy that arises when believers are united by the Holy Spirit. The Spirit draws us together, and in that unity, we experience the joy of shared faith, shared purpose, and shared worship. This is why gathering with other believers is so important—our joy is often magnified in community, as the Spirit moves among us.

MAINTAINING JOY THROUGH THE HOLY SPIRIT

Finally, maintaining joy in the Holy Spirit requires that we stay connected to Him. The Bible encourages us not to quench the Spirit (1 Thessalonians 5:19) or grieve Him (Ephesians 4:30). When we neglect our relationship with God, ignore the Spirit's leading, or allow sin to take root in our lives, our joy can diminish. However, when we are sensitive to the Spirit's voice, obedient to His guidance, and committed to nurturing our relationship with Him, joy flourishes.

Practical ways to maintain joy in the Holy Spirit include spending time in prayer, meditating on God's Word, worshiping, and staying in fellowship with other believers. The more we cultivate our relationship with the Spirit, the more His joy fills our hearts.

CONCLUSION: EMBRACING THE JOY OF THE HOLY SPIRIT

> The Spirit brings us into the presence of God, empowers us for life, leads us into truth, and unites us with other believers.

Finding joy in the Holy Spirit is not a mystery—it is the natural result of living in relationship with Him. The Spirit brings us into the presence of God, empowers us for life, leads us into truth, and unites us with other believers. His joy is steadfast, enduring, and available to us in every season of life. As we walk with the Holy Spirit, we can experience a deep, abiding joy that cannot be shaken by circumstances.

May we learn to live each day filled with the Holy Spirit, embracing the joy He offers as we journey with Him.

> **JOY BUILDER TIP:**
>
> Try to meet up with a close friend for coffee or tea or whatever you prefer. Pick one Scripture that speaks to both of you. Fellowship and share your thoughts on that Scripture.

CHAPTER 18
CRUSH YOUR IDOL/S BEFORE IT CRUSHES YOU

You shall have no other gods before me. You shall not make for yourself a carved image, or any likeness of anything that is in heaven above, or that is in the earth beneath, or that is in the water under the earth. You shall not bow down to them or serve them, for I the LORD your God am a jealous God, visiting the iniquity of the fathers on the children to the third and the fourth generation of those who hate me, but showing steadfast love to thousands of those who love me and keep my commandments. Exodus 20:3-6

As I started writing this chapter, I searched for the Biblical definition of idolatry. Although there were a few variances this one really hits home

"The worship of someone or something other than God as though it were God"

Anytime I think of the topic of idolatry I can't help but to think of one of my favorite Biblical Stories of all time. It's starts in Daniel Chapter 3. Before we dive in let me start by saying this. I love Daniel. I love Daniel in the lions den. I love Daniel interpreting dreams and most of all I love him prophesying about our great Savior. With that said though sadly these 3 men I am about to talk about to me personally I don't think they get enough attention. Everyone seems to always talk about Daniel. But what about his 3 best friends who did the unthinkable. I am speaking of none other than Shadrach Meshach and Abednego. To save us all some time from here on aside from the Scriptures I will refer to them as SMA. I hope they don't mind. So let's jump in. The scene starts at Daniel 3 4-7

"Then the herald loudly proclaimed, "Nations and peoples of every language, this is what you are commanded to do: As soon as you hear the sound of the horn, flute, zither, lyre, harp, pipe and all kinds of music, you must fall down and worship the Image of gold that King Nebuchadnezzar has set up. Whoever does not fall down and worship will immediately be thrown into a blazing furnace."

"Therefore, as soon as they heard the sound of the horn, flute, zither, lyre, harp and all kinds of music, all the nations and peoples of every language fell down and worshiped the image of gold that King Nebuchadnezzar had set up."

> We have a Big God who is greater than any statue, anyone or anything.

The herald and King Nebuchadnezzar's command was very straight forward. To simplify. "Either bow down to my statue or die". As we journey through this story please ponder what your "statue" is. It doesn't have to be made of gold or bronze. It could be our cellphones, another person, a habit, even a good thing that we put before God. Fill in the blank.

No condemnation whatsoever but if we are being honest we all have a statue or two in our lives. But that's okay because we have a Big God who is greater than any statue, anyone or anything. Let us continue the story. "

> Anytime tragedy strikes in our world, I believe us Christians are the first looked at to see how we respond.

At this time some astrologers[a] came forward and denounced the Jews. They said to King Nebuchadnezzar, "May the king live forever! Your Majesty has issued a decree that everyone who hears the sound of the horn, flute, zither, lyre, harp, pipe and all kinds of music must fall down and worship the image of gold, 11 and that whoever does not fall down and worship will be thrown into a blazing furnace. But there are some Jews whom you have set over the affairs of the province of Babylon—Shadrach, Meshach and Abednego—who pay no attention to you, Your Majesty. They neither serve your gods nor worship the image of gold you have set up."

> We have such a good Father that no matter how far we stray, His arms are always open waiting for us to come back home.

Please keep in mind this wasn't some small show at the Apollo. The Bible literally says every nation with every language was there. For my older friends this would make Woodstock look like WhatStock? Needless to say this was a big deal. Also on a side note it is very interesting to know that all nations were there and these kings men were able to spot out 3 teenage Jewish kids not bowing down. I am by no means adding to the Bible. But it's almost as if they were purposely looking for them to screw up. Sound familiar? Anytime tragedy strikes in our world, I believe us Christians are the first looked at to see how we respond. "let's see how those Christians handle this" oh Lord if they only knew the problems we have as well. But anyways not to get sidetracked. We may read this story many times. And just like all Bible stories, we have to remind ourselves these are not just some fairytales. These things really happened. Could you imagine being SMA. Three teenagers who literally have the whole world watching them to shortly be thrown into a blazing furnace for not bowing down to a statue? Like we may have done, they could have easily went along with the world's ways just to fit in or be in the popular crowd thinking "oh God understands I didn't really mean it. I'll just bow down and ask Him to forgive me after" More times that I'd like to admit, I've been part of that cycle too. But please don't leave me hanging. I think some of you if not most can relate. By no means am I endorsing license to sin or to commit idolatry by saying this. Far be it from me. But I believe and more importantly ,the Bible says when we confess our sins He is faithful and just to forgive us for them. However I will say the more we continue this cycle we will not experience the fullness of His goodness and grace and it will definitely hinder our walk. But with that said it is such a great comfort that we have such a good Father that no matter how far we stray, His arms are always open waiting for us to come back home. But this wasn't so with SMA. They are the perfect example of complete obedience without hesitation. The Bible goes on to say.

"Furious with rage, Nebuchadnezzar summoned Shadrach, Meshach and Abednego. So these men were brought before the king, 14 and Nebuchadnezzar said to them, "Is it true, Shadrach, Meshach and Abednego, that you do not serve my gods or worship the image of gold I have set up? Now when you hear the sound of the horn, flute, zither, lyre, harp, pipe and all kinds of music, if you are ready to fall down and worship the image I made, very good. But if you do not worship it, you will be thrown immediately into a blazing furnace. Then what god will be able to rescue you from my hand?" Daniel 3:13-15.

Again, they could have easily told a "white lie". Knowing they failed but God would forgive them. If we are being completely honest how many of us would have possibly done so and justified our disobedience? It has been well said that partial obedience is not obedience at all. But come on, they were literally about to be thrown in a blazing furnace of fire for simply not bowing down to some stupid statue that meant nothing to them anyway? The statue may have meant nothing to them. But their allegiance to God did and meant everything to them! Let us remember no matter how great our Idols are or make us feel they will always always in the end let you down. But I believe it can be a great thing when someone or something let's you down because it reminds you to look up. We read.

CRUSH YOUR IDOL/S BEFORE IT CRUSHES YOU

> It can be a great thing when someone or something let's you down because it reminds you to look up.

"Shadrach, Meshach and Abednego replied to him, "King Nebuchadnezzar, we do not need to defend ourselves before you in this matter. If we are thrown into the blazing furnace, the God we serve is able to deliver us from it, and he will deliver us[c] from Your Majesty's hand. But even if he does not, we want you to know, Your Majesty, that we will not serve your gods or worship the image of gold you have set up."
Daniel 3:16-18

I don't know about you but every time I read those words it sends chills down my spine! Of course in a God way.

The God we serve is able to deliver us from it, and he will deliver us[c] from Your Majesty's hand. But even if he does not, we want you to know, Your Majesty, that we will not serve your gods or worship the image of gold you have set up."

> The God we serve is able to deliver us from it, and he will deliver us[c] from Your Majesty's hand. But even if he does not, we want you to know, Your Majesty, that we will not serve your gods or worship the image of gold you have set up."

"But even if He does not"?!. Personally some of the bravest words in the Bible. Of course nothing like our great Savior in the garden. But with basically the exact same point. When Jesus says

Father, if you are willing, take this cup from me; yet not my will, but yours be done."
Luke 22:42

Of course like I said earlier Jesus is our greatest example. And we also know Jesus did end up suffering for all the sins of the world for you and me. But what great faith SMA had?! Three teenage Jewish boys who were so faithful and dedicated to the Father that even if God does not save them, they would not only not bow down to the statue but were also ready to be thrown into a fiery furnace. But as we will see later as with you brave warrior God will always reward your faithfulness in any fiery furnace you may currently be dealing with.

We read on

Then Nebuchadnezzar was furious with Shadrach, Meshach and Abednego, and his attitude toward them changed. He ordered the furnace heated seven times hotter than usual and commanded some of the strongest soldiers in his army to tie up Shadrach, Meshach and Abednego and throw them into the blazing furnace. So these men, wearing their robes, trousers, turbans and other clothes, were bound and thrown into the blazing furnace.

Daniel 3:19-21

As I mentioned earlier, this was not some tall tale. These events actually happened with real people let alone young kids.

I ask you to reflect on what fiery furnace you may be dealing with at this time. Maybe a loss of a job? Your health? Loss of a loved one? Even though those things are horrible and we are in the midst of the fire of life, is it possible that we are not alone? What if there was another Man in the fire with us. Is it possible we could survive the flames? Let us read on

The king's command was so urgent and the furnace so hot that the flames of the fire killed the soldiers who took up Shadrach, Meshach and Abednego, 23 and these three men, firmly tied, fell into the blazing furnace.

Then King Nebuchadnezzar leaped to his feet in amazement and asked his advisers, "Weren't there three men that we tied up and threw into the fire?"

They replied, "Certainly, Your Majesty."

He said, "Look! I see four men walking around in the fire, unbound and unharmed, and the fourth looks like a son of the gods."

Daniel 3:22-25

> If you take away anything from this story please let it be that no matter what fire you may be standing in no matter how hot it may be, that there is another Man in the fire with you.

I believe Nebuchadnezzar was close but a little off. He said I see a fourth man in the fire who looks like "a" "son" of God. But I believe with all my heart that it was "The" "Son" of God. Our Lord and Savior Jesus Christ. What most theologians call a foreshadowing of our Savior. If you take away anything from this story please let it be that no matter what fire you may be standing in no matter how hot it may be, that there is another Man in the fire with you. Who says to you He will never leave you or forsake you. So much so that like SMA by the grace of God you can walk out of this fire not even smelling like smoke! Your hair won't be singed and even your clothes not burned. All because of the One who is standing in the fire with you!

> Even the smell of smoke was not on them

The satraps, the prefects, the governors and the king's counselors gathered around them and saw that in regard to these men the fire had no effect on their bodies—their hair was not singed, their clothes were not scorched or damaged, even the smell of smoke was not on them.

Daniel 3:27

> **JOY BUILDER TIP:**
>
> This is a tough one but the reward will be worth it. We should never give for the intention of getting blessed. But when we give out of our heart. God does definitely bless us and this will significantly increase your joy. Pick one item that is sentimental to you and give to the person that God has put on your heart lately. As Jesus said it is better to give than to receive Acts 20:35

CHAPTER 19

THE JOY OF PRAYER: A HEARTFELT CONVERSATION

INTRODUCTION

Prayer is one of the most intimate ways we connect with God, yet for many, it can feel daunting or routine. However, when we shift our perspective from viewing prayer as a chore to embracing it as a joyous conversation with our Creator, we open ourselves up to an experience filled with love, gratitude, and spiritual growth.

1. UNDERSTANDING THE PURPOSE OF PRAYER

> Prayer is one of the most intimate ways we connect with God

Before diving into the joy of prayer, it's important to understand its purpose. Prayer serves as a powerful means to communicate with God. It allows us to express our thoughts, concerns, and gratitude. In Philippians 4:6-7, we are reminded,

"Do not be anxious about anything, but in every situation, by prayer and petition, with thanksgiving, present your requests to God."

This scripture beautifully encapsulates the idea that prayer is not solely about asking for things but about cultivating a relationship built on trust and openness.

2. SHIFTING OUR MINDSET

> When we engage in heartfelt dialogue with God, we become aware of His presence surrounding us.

Many of us have been taught that prayer should be eloquent and formal. However, God desires authenticity over perfection. Approach prayer like you would with a close friend. Share your worries, joys, and even doubts. In Matthew 6:7, Jesus advises us to avoid "babbling like pagans," reminding us that sincerity in conversation is what truly matters.

When we set aside our expectations and simply speak from the heart, we create an atmosphere where joy can flourish. It becomes less about the right words and more about the right attitude—a willingness to be vulnerable and open with the One who knows us best.

3. FINDING JOY IN COMMUNING WITH GOD

Consider the moments in your life where your heart felt the lightness of joy. Often, these instances arise when we experience genuine connection, laughter, and love. The same can be said for prayer. When we engage in heartfelt dialogue with God, we become aware of His presence surrounding us.

Try incorporating a few practices that can elevate your prayer life:

- **Gratitude Journaling**: Start each prayer by listing a few things you are thankful for. This practice shifts the focus from our needs to recognizing God's goodness in our lives. Gratitude opens the door to joy.

- **Listening:** Prayer is a two-way street. Spend time in silence after your requests, allowing God to speak to your heart. Reflecting on His answers can reignite your joy and faith.

- **Adoration:** Spend time praising God for who He is. Acknowledge His love, mercy, and power. This focus on God's nature can lift our spirits and fill our hearts with joy.

4. ENGAGING IN PRAYER THROUGHOUT YOUR DAY

> Joy in prayer isn't limited to formal times of devotion. It can permeate every moment of our day.

Joy in prayer isn't limited to formal times of devotion. It can permeate every moment of our day. We can invite God into mundane tasks, turning ordinary moments into opportunities for connection. Whether you're commuting, running errands, or working on a project, include God in your thoughts. Simple prayers like, "Thank You for this day, Lord," or "Guide me as I work," weave prayer into your daily life.

As we continually communicate with God, we grow in our awareness of His presence, which fuels our joy.

5. THE JOY OF INTERCESSION

One of the most beautiful aspects of prayer is intercession—lifting others up to God. When we pray for friends, family, or even strangers, we align our hearts with God's will and purposes. This selflessness fosters joy, as we become conduits of God's love and grace.

Engage in specific intercessory prayer, seeking out those in need and bringing them before the Lord. The joy you experience when you see God answer those prayers, or simply knowing you've contributed to someone's spiritual journey, is profound.

CONCLUSION

Finding joy in prayer is a journey of deepening our relationship with God. As we focus on authenticity, gratitude, and the simple act of communicating with our Creator, we begin to taste the sweetness of His presence.

Prayer is not just about seeking answers but about building a loving relationship that overflows with joy. May we embrace the call to pray with hearts wide open, finding joy in the conversations we hold with the One who loves us endlessly.

As you move forward in your prayer life, remember that every prayer is an opportunity to connect with joy, and every moment spent in God's presence will enrich your spirit in ways you never imagined. Give yourself permission to enjoy this sacred gift—one heartfelt prayer at a time.

> **JOY BUILDER TIP:**
>
> If you are out and about. Ask as many people possible that you encounter if you could pray for them. Pray for them on the spot. As I shamefully admit myself at times but I believe all of us have been guilty of it at some point or another. When we tell someone we will pray for them. Then when we pray we totally forget. With this tip. I definitely recommend testing the spirits as the Bible says as not everyone might be as welcoming. Ask the Holy Spirit to help you discern

CHAPTER 20

DON'T LET THE DEVIL STEAL YOUR JOY

The thief comes only to steal and kill and destroy; I came that they may have life and have it abundantly
John 10:10

> There is no such thing as true joy other than through our Great Savior Jesus Christ.

First of all if you have come this far in your battle for joy, you are a true warrior. I am beyond proud of you and far more importantly I believe God has a smile on His face as well, knowing that His children are trying to seek Him with all their hearts and fighting for the joy that is so graciously bestowed upon us. Through Him and from Him only. There is no such thing as true joy other than through our Great Savior Jesus Christ. As we continue on our mission let us take a trip into the wilderness with our great Savior before His mission on earth began. To overcome the devil and his schemes it is best that we learn from the One who has overcome all. Because as the Scriptures say

> *Greater is He(God big H) who is in us than he(satan little h) that is in the world*
> **1 John 4:4(emphasis added)**

Before we dive into the wilderness it is very important to know what took place right before. Matthew 3:16-17 says this

And Jesus, when he was baptized, went up straightway out of the water: and, lo, the heavens were opened unto him, and he saw the Spirit of God descending like a dove, and lighting upon him:

And lo a voice from heaven, saying, This is my beloved Son, in whom I am well pleased.

As we know after Jesus was baptized this was God's public declaration and approval of His Son. Please notice that God was well pleased with Jesus "before" His mission even begun.

So for those of us who are caught in the cycle of performance to please God. Meditate on that verse. There is nothing you can do for God to love you more than He already does. Please don't get me wrong though, we definitely still a mission and kingdom purpose. But we don't do those things to get God to love us. We do things because like the Word says

We love God because he first loved us.

1 John 4:19

With that said, let us take a walk in the wilderness for the biggest showdown in history.

> *Then was Jesus led up of the Spirit into the wilderness to be tempted of the devil.*
> **Matthew 4:1**

It is very interesting to know that the Spirit led Jesus into

The wilderness. But it is very important that we understand that God does not tempt us but He definitely does test us.

Let no one say when he is tempted, "I am tempted by God"; for God cannot be tempted by evil, nor does He Himself tempt anyone

James 1:13

But God loves us so much that He will allow us to come to the end of ourselves only to lift us up to become our true selves in Him.

> But God loves us so much that He will allow us to come to the end of ourselves only to lift us up to become our true selves in Him.

For whom the LORD loves He chastens, And scourges every son whom He receives." Hebrews 12:6

Let us read on

He fasted for forty days and forty nights,* and afterwards he was hungry. The tempter approached and said to him, "If you are the Son of God, command that these stones become loaves of bread."

Matthew 4:2-3

Notice the first thing the devil asked Jesus.

"If You are the Son of God?" Again keep in mind this is right after Jesus's "public" Baptism where the Father literally says "this is my Son. In Him I am well pleased". Needless to say the devil knew what he was doing. He tried to attack Jesus's identity. And so he does with us. Because the moment we lose our identity in Christ is the moment we lose the battle.

We will try to fight in our own strength and will never win.

So please never forget in spiritual warfare and life in general what the Scripture says

For you died, and your life is now hidden with Christ in God

Colossians 3:3

Let us continue with the battle. Notice after the devil attacked Christ's identity and also tried to make Him act outside the will of the Father. That our Lord did not for one second converse with the enemy or truly consider his temptations other than rebuking it. Without hesitation Jesus fought back with The Word of God

But he answered, 'It is written,

'Man shall not live by bread alone, but by every word that proceeds from the mouth of God. '"
Matthew 4:4

> If Jesus the Son Of God used The Word, how much more should we use it?

It is safe to say that Jesus studied, meditated and mulled over the Word in His heart so much so that it was ready to flow out of Him in any occasion. Especially one like this. This He used from Deuteronomy 8:3 That is why it is so crucial to do the same. If Jesus the Son Of God used The Word, how much more should we use it?

After this the devil takes it up a notch

Then the devil took him to the holy city and had him stand on the highest point of the temple. "If you are the Son of God," he said, "throw yourself down. For it is written: " 'He will command his angels concerning you, and they will lift you up in their hands, so that you will not strike your foot against a stone.

Matthew 4:5-6

We see here that the devil uses Scripture himself. I hate to say but he probably knows it better than most of us. However with that being said. Nowhere in the Bible does he ever use it properly. Please take note that here he is quoting from

Psalm 91:10-12

For he will command his angels concerning you to guard you in all your ways; they will lift you up in their hands, so that you will not strike your foot against a stone.

Notice that the devil left out a very important part of that verse. "For he will command his angels concerning you to guard you in "all" your ways (emphasis added) . So could have Jesus jumped down and the Father would send angels to guard Him and keep Him from falling? Absolutely. But if He did jump would He be acting outside the will of the Father? Again I say absolutely. That is why it so important we understand the Word in the right context. Because sadly as Satan did a great many have used it out of context to deceive many. Once again let us see how our Great Lord deals with this second temptation.

Jesus answered him,

> *"Again it is written, 'You shall not put the Lord, your God, to the test. '*
> ***Matthew 4:7-8***

Here we see once again. Jesus did not debate with Satan or give his words any power. But again without hesitation, He fired back with "it is written" Jesus got this verse from Deuteronomy 6:16

Again I cannot pound the point home enough that the only way to destroy the devil and his lies is through The Word of God with the help of His of His Holy Spirit. Of course there are some other things in- between. But when it really comes down to it. We really only all need three things in our walk with Christ and life in general. The Word Of God, The Holy Spirit and me and you. The Church. I believe one of our biggest issues with spiritual warfare and in life, is that I don't think we always fully realize or believe in what power we have in the Word! Myself definitely included. But the Word testifies of itself in Hebrews 4:12 that says

For the word of God is living and powerful, sharper than any two-edged sword, piercing to the division of soul and of spirit, of joints and of marrow, and discerning the thoughts and intentions of the heart.

We literally have in the Bibles we carry around the greatest power known and that is God and is Word. But in order to harness that power we must use it. It makes me think definitely of myself and I'm sure some if not most of you as well. Think about how many apps we have on our phone. Some of these apps can truly do some amazing things. But I then ask this question. When was the last time you utilized those apps. That like most of us got so excited when we first heard about it and downloaded only to totally forget about it a week later and never harness it's full power? And so it is with The Word of God. The greatest "App" ever created! Don't get me wrong I am by no means condemning. I am fully guilty of this myself at times. However I am by the Holy Spirit trying to fire you up to dive into The Word like never before! Pull out that weapon and use it. That is the only way we will silence the lies of the devil and win every war we ever fight! Like Jesus half brother James says

But don't just listen to God's word. You must do what it says. Otherwise, you are only fooling yourself

James 1:22

Let us go now to the third and last temptation of the Lord in the wilderness

Again, the devil took him to a very high mountain and showed him all the kingdoms of the world and their splendor. "All this I will give you," he said, "if you will bow down and worship me." Jesus said to him, "Away from me, Satan! For it Is written: 'Worship the Lord your God, and serve him only.

Matthew 4:8

First of all Satan is the father of all lies(Romans 8:44) so we don't even know for sure if he possessed all he offered and more importantly even if he did, I don't trust him giving it away. Although he is the god. Little G of this world. Please don't get me wrong I do not say this at all to minimize the temptation of our Lord. Even if it was a lie, Jesus was at one of His most vulnerable spots. I've heard this well said acronym that will definitely help us in times of warfare and life. H.A.L.T. Hungry, Angry, Lonely and tired if you are any or all of those things. Please keep in mind that is where you are most likely susceptible to give into temptation and a whole host of other things.

JOY BUILDER TIP:

Every time the devil sends one of his fiery darts(thoughts) at you. Say Greater is He(big H) who is in me, than he(little h) who is in the world.

CHAPTER 21

FINDING JOY IN THE PRESENCE OF THE FATHER

INTRODUCTION

> *You make known to me the path of life;*
> *You will fill me with joy in your presence,*
> *With eternal pleasures at your right hand.*
> **Psalm 16:11**

> Within the presence of God lies a boundless well of joy that is waiting for us to tap into.

In our fast-paced world filled with noise and distractions, it often feels challenging to find moments of joy and peace. Yet, within the presence of God lies a boundless well of joy that is waiting for us to tap into. When we intentionally seek His presence, we not only experience joy but also discover a profound sense of purpose, love, and connection. This chapter will explore how we can find joy in God's presence and the transformative power it brings to our lives.

1. UNDERSTANDING GOD'S PRESENCE

To find joy in God's presence, we must first understand what it means to be in His presence. Throughout scripture, we are reminded that God is always near. Psalm 139:7-10 tells us, "Where can I go from Your Spirit? Where can I flee from Your presence?" This powerful declaration reassures us that no matter where we are or what we are experiencing, God is with us. Understanding this omnipresence can bring comfort and encourage us to seek His presence in every moment.

2. THE INVITATION TO ABIDE

> God invites us to abide in Him—an intentional choice to dwell in relationship with Him

God invites us to abide in Him—an intentional choice to dwell in relationship with Him. In John 15:4, Jesus says,

"Remain in Me, and I will remain in you."

Abiding involves cultivating a deep, personal relationship that is marked by trust and intimacy. As we draw closer to God, we begin to experience His joy more profoundly.

Consider taking intentional steps to foster this connection:

- **Daily Time with God:** Set aside time daily for prayer, reading scripture, and simply being in God's presence. This creates a rhythm of communion with the Lord.

- **Silence and Solitude**: In the stillness of silence, we can hear God's voice clearer, and in that space, we can discover an overwhelming sense of peace and joy.

- **Meditation on His Word**: Reflecting on scripture can anchor our thoughts and open our hearts to the joy found in the truth of His promises. Focus on verses that highlight His love, provision, and faithfulness.

3. THE JOY OF WORSHIP

> When we worship—whether through music, art, or acts of service—we turn our hearts towards Him

Worship is a powerful way to invite God's presence into our lives. When we worship—whether through music, art, or acts of service—we turn our hearts towards Him. Psalm 100:2 encourages us to

> *"Worship the Lord with gladness; come before Him with joyful songs."*

In these moments of worship, we align ourselves with God's heart and uncover the joy that comes from glorifying Him.

Consider the following:

- **Create a Worship Space**: Set up a specific area in your home where you can express your worship freely. Fill it with reminders of God's goodness—scripture, art, or cherished memories.

- **Engage in Community Worship**: Participating in worship within a community can amplify the joy we experience together. The collective praise creates an atmosphere of celebration and connection.

> Gratitude is a key that opens the door to joy

4. THE GIFT OF GRATITUDE

Gratitude is a key that opens the door to joy. When we intentionally choose to thank God for His blessings, we acknowledge His goodness and cultivate a joyful heart. In 1 Thessalonians 5:16-18, we are encouraged to

> *"Rejoice always, pray continually, give thanks in all circumstances; for this is God's will for you in Christ Jesus."*

To practice gratitude in God's presence:

- **Keep a Gratitude Journal**: List daily blessings, big and small. Reflecting on these gifts can help shift your perspective, revealing the abundance of joy in your life.
- **Share Your Gratitude**: Express thanks to God in prayers and share your gratitude with others. This not only spreads joy but also strengthens your bond with the community.

5. THE TRANSFORMATIVE POWER OF JOY

Joy is not just a fleeting emotion; it is a fruit of the Spirit (Galatians 5:22). When we cultivate joy in God's presence, it transforms how we perceive challenges, relationships, and even ourselves. Joy allows us to rise above our circumstances, reassuring us of God's constant love and grace.

> As we nourish our hearts with joy, it spills over into our interactions with others

As we nourish our hearts with joy, it spills over into our interactions with others. We become vessels of joy reflecting God's love to the world around us.

CONCLUSION

Finding joy in the presence of God is a journey of faith, intentionality, and willingness to connect with our Creator. By understanding His abiding presence, engaging in worship, practicing gratitude, and embracing joy as a spiritual gift, we unlock a deeper relationship with God and discover a joy that transcends circumstances.

As you move forward, remember that each moment spent in God's presence holds the potential for joy. Seek Him earnestly, and you will find that in His embrace, joy awaits—a joy that not only uplifts your spirit but also transforms your entire life. Let the joy of His presence fill your heart and overflow into every aspect of your journey, leading you to a life marked by hope, purpose, and unshakeable joy.

> ### JOY BUILDER TIP:
>
> For your next personal Bible Study, grab a concordance and look up all Scripture that talks about joy. As you study, pick out your favorite one and meditate on it throughout the week.

CHAPTER 22
JOY IN HAVING THE MIND OF CHRIST

For who has known the mind of the Lord, that he may instruct Him? But we have the mind of Christ.".
1 Corinthians 2:16

INTRODUCTION

In the journey of Christian faith, one of the most profound transformations is the renewal of our minds. When we receive Christ, we are called not only to imitate His actions but also to adopt His mindset. The Apostle Paul emphasized this in Philippians 2:5,

> *"Let this mind be in you which was also in Christ Jesus."*

This transformation is more than just a change in behavior; it is a change in the way we perceive, think, and respond to life. One of the greatest blessings of this transformation is the deep and abiding joy that flows from having the mind of Christ.

This joy is not a fleeting emotion, dependent on circumstances. Rather, it is a steady undercurrent of peace, contentment, and fulfillment that comes from aligning our thoughts with God's will and purpose. In this chapter, we will explore the nature of the mind of Christ, how it produces joy in the believer, and the practical steps we can take to cultivate and experience this joy.

1. The Nature of the Mind of Christ

The mind of Christ is characterized by humility, obedience, love, and peace. In Philippians 2:6-8, Paul describes Christ's mindset:

> "Who, being in very nature God, did not consider equality with God something to be used to his own advantage; rather, he made himself nothing by taking the very nature of a servant, being made in human likeness. And being found in appearance as a man, he humbled himself by becoming obedient to death—even death on a cross!"

This passage reveals several key attributes of Christ's mind:

Humility: Christ did not cling to His divine status but humbled Himself to serve humanity. Humility is essential to having the mind of Christ because it frees us from pride, which often blocks the flow of joy in our lives.

Obedience: Jesus was obedient to the will of the Father, even when it led to suffering. Obedience brings joy because it aligns us with God's perfect plan, which is always for our ultimate good.

Love: Christ's mindset is one of sacrificial love. Joy flows from love because when we love others selflessly, we experience the fulfillment of living as God intended.

Peace: The mind of Christ is free from anxiety, trusting completely in the Father. This trust results in peace, which is a critical foundation for lasting joy.

2. The Joy That Flows from the Mind of Christ

When we embrace the mind of Christ, we experience a profound joy that is rooted in God Himself. This joy is not dependent on external circumstances but is a result of our internal transformation. Several aspects of this joy include:

The Joy of Humility: Humility is often misunderstood as weakness, but in Christ, humility is a source of strength. When we humble ourselves before God, we release the burden of pride and ego, which often leads to stress, frustration, and disappointment. In humility, we find joy in knowing that we are loved and accepted by God, not because of our accomplishments, but because of His grace.

The Joy of Obedience: Obeying God can sometimes be challenging, especially when His will seems to conflict with our desires. However, obedience to God leads to joy because it brings us into alignment with His perfect plan. Jesus said in John 15:10-11,

"If you keep my commands, you will remain in my love, just as I have kept my Father's commands and remain in his love. I have told you this so that my joy may be in you and that your joy may be complete."

Complete joy comes from walking in obedience to God's will.

The Joy of Love: The mind of Christ is filled with love for God and others. When we adopt His mindset, we experience the joy of living in loving relationships. Jesus taught that loving others is one of the greatest commandments (Mark 12:30-31), and it is through loving others that we experience the fullness of joy. As 1 John 4:12 states,

> *"If we love one another, God abides in us, and His love has been perfected in us."*

Joy flourishes when we live in the love of Christ.

The Joy of Peace: Peace is the absence of inner turmoil. When we trust in God and surrender our anxieties to Him, we experience the peace that surpasses understanding (Philippians 4:7). This peace brings joy because it allows us to rest in God's sovereignty, knowing that He is in control of all things, even when life is uncertain or difficult.

3. Cultivating the Mind of Christ

While the transformation of our minds begins with the work of the Holy Spirit, there are practical steps we can take to cultivate and maintain the mind of Christ, thereby increasing our joy. These steps include:

Renewing Our Minds with God's Word: Romans 12:2 instructs us,

"Do not conform to the pattern of this world, but be transformed by the renewing of your mind."

We renew our minds by immersing ourselves in Scripture, allowing God's truth to shape our thoughts, attitudes, and beliefs.

Practicing Gratitude: Gratitude is a powerful way to cultivate joy. When we focus on the blessings in our lives, we shift our mindset from one of lack to one of abundance. Philippians 4:6-7 encourages us to present our requests to God with thanksgiving, and in doing so, we experience His peace and joy.

Serving Others: Jesus demonstrated the joy of servanthood. When we serve others, we reflect the heart of Christ and experience the joy that comes from giving rather than receiving. Acts 20:35 reminds us that

"It is more blessed to give than to receive."

Living in Fellowship: The Christian life is not meant to be lived in isolation. Fellowship with other believers encourages us and strengthens our faith. In community, we can share our joys, bear each other's burdens, and grow together in the likeness of Christ.

Prayer and Meditation: Maintaining an active prayer life helps us stay connected to God and grounded in His presence. When we meditate on His Word and communicate with Him regularly, we invite His joy to fill our hearts.

4. The Eternal Joy in Christ

Finally, the joy of having the mind of Christ extends beyond this life. It is a joy rooted in the eternal hope of being with Him forever. Jesus endured the cross

> *"for the joy that was set before Him"*
> ***(Hebrews 12:2).***

That same joy is ours, knowing that our present sufferings are temporary and that eternal glory awaits us. This eternal perspective fills us with joy even in the midst of trials because we know that God is working all things for our good (Romans 8:28).

CONCLUSION

The joy that comes from having the mind of Christ is deep, lasting, and transformative. It is a joy that transcends circumstances and is rooted in the character and purposes of God. By embracing humility, obedience, love, and peace, and by renewing our minds through His Word, we can experience the fullness of joy that Christ offers. As we continue to cultivate His mindset, we will discover that true joy is found not in what we have or do, but in who we are becoming in Him.

JOY BUILDER TIP:

As long as your finances allow it and it is appropriate buy one nice thing for yourself. It doesn't have to be expensive. It's okay to have some nice things as long as they don't have us!

CHAPTER 23
THE JOY OF NEVER GIVING UP

The journey of faith is often depicted as a battle—a struggle not against flesh and blood, but against doubt, despair, and the trials that challenge our belief. In this life, we face constant obstacles that try to dim the light of faith within us, and it can be tempting to give up when the road gets tough. Yet, as Christians, we are called to stand firm, not only enduring the trials of faith but doing so with joy. This joy, grounded in Christ, is not the fleeting happiness that depends on circumstances, but a deep, abiding joy that sustains us even in the hardest battles.

THE NATURE OF THE FIGHT

The Apostle Paul described the Christian life as a race and a fight (2 Timothy 4:7). He knew firsthand the hardships of faith, from shipwrecks and imprisonments to beatings and betrayals. But Paul didn't back down from the fight. Why? Because he understood that faith was worth fighting for—faith connects us to the God who never leaves nor forsakes us.

> Faith is not simply a mental exercise. It is a battle of the heart, a daily decision to trust in God's promises over what we see and feel

Faith is not simply a mental exercise. It is a battle of the heart, a daily decision to trust in God's promises over what we see and feel. It is choosing to believe that God is good even when life seems unfair, that He is present even when we feel alone, and that He is working all things together for good, even when we can't see the full picture.

This fight is often waged in the quiet moments of life—when doubts creep in, when prayers seem unanswered, or when suffering persists. The enemy whispers that it's easier to give up, to coast, or to stop trying. But the Bible reminds us that the

> *"testing of your faith produces perseverance"*
> **(James 1:3).**

Perseverance isn't passive endurance; it is active, forward-moving faith that presses on because it knows that the prize is worth the struggle.

CHRISTIAN JOY: OUR STRENGTH IN THE FIGHT

> *"Do not grieve, for the joy of the Lord is your strength"*
> **(Nehemiah 8:10).**

Christian joy is a weapon in the fight for faith. It's not just an emotion; it's a posture of the heart, rooted in the reality of God's goodness and faithfulness. This joy comes from knowing that no matter what comes our way, God is sovereign, He is loving, and He is with us.

The world often equates joy with happiness, but Christian joy runs deeper. It's the joy that Jesus spoke of when He said,

> *"I have told you this so that my joy may be in you and that your joy may be complete"*
> **(John 15:11).**

His joy is full, complete, and enduring. It isn't based on external circumstances but on an internal reality—the reality that we are loved, redeemed, and held by God Himself.

> His joy is full, complete, and enduring. It isn't based on external circumstances but on an internal reality—the reality that we are loved, redeemed, and held by God Himself.

One of the greatest examples of joy in the midst of struggle is found in the life of Jesus. Hebrews 12:2 tells us that

"for the joy set before him, he endured the cross, scorning its shame."

Jesus' joy was not in the agony of the cross, but in the outcome—the redemption of humanity and the fulfillment of God's plan. His joy was anchored in the assurance that His suffering had a purpose, that His Father's will was perfect, and that beyond the pain lay eternal victory.

CHOOSING JOY IN TRIALS

How can we maintain joy in the face of trials? The answer lies in where we place our focus. If we focus on the problem, our joy will wane. But if we focus on the promises of God, our joy can flourish even in the darkest valleys.

James 1:2-4 gives us a profound perspective:

"Consider it pure joy, my brothers and sisters, whenever you face trials of many kinds, because you know that the testing of your faith produces perseverance. Let perseverance finish its work so that you may be mature and complete, not lacking anything."

James is not telling us to enjoy pain or suffering. Rather, he encourages us to have joy in knowing that God is working through our trials to mature our faith. Every hardship becomes an opportunity to grow, to draw nearer to God, and to experience His sustaining power.

One way to cultivate joy is through thanksgiving. When we focus on what we have, rather than what we lack, we remind our hearts of God's faithfulness. Paul, writing from prison, instructed the Philippians to "rejoice in the Lord always" (Philippians 4:4). His circumstances were grim, but his joy came from knowing Christ. Even in chains, Paul could give thanks because his joy was in the Lord, not in his situation.

FAITH WITH JOY: A TESTIMONY TO THE WORLD

> When we fight the battle of faith with joy, we offer a powerful testimony to the world. In a world filled with fear, anxiety, and hopelessness, a Christian who exudes joy stands out.

When we fight the battle of faith with joy, we offer a powerful testimony to the world. In a world filled with fear, anxiety, and hopelessness, a Christian who exudes joy stands out. It is this joy, unshaken by circumstances, that draws people to Christ. When others see us rejoicing in the midst of trials, they see a reflection of the hope we have in Jesus.

Peter writes that believers are

"filled with an inexpressible and glorious joy"
(1 Peter 1:8)

because of our faith in Jesus. This joy is a witness that our hope is not in the temporary, but in the eternal. It points to the reality that God is with us, that He has a plan, and that He is trustworthy.

THE ULTIMATE VICTORY

The fight for faith is not without reward. Paul declared,

> *"I have fought the good fight, I have finished the race, I have kept the faith. Now there is in store for me the crown of righteousness"*
> ***(2 Timothy 4:7-8).***

The crown of righteousness is the reward for those who persevere. But the ultimate victory isn't merely in the future—it's also in the present. Every day that we choose faith over fear, every time we choose joy in the face of trials, we experience a foretaste of the victory that is ours in Christ.

God has not left us to fight alone. He has given us His Spirit to strengthen, comfort, and guide us. He has given us His Word to remind us of His promises. And He has given us His joy—a joy that sustains us, empowers us, and propels us forward in the fight for faith.

CONCLUSION: PRESSING ON

> We press on because we know that the God who began a good work in us will carry it on to completion

As Christians, we are called to fight the good fight of faith. But this is not a fight we enter alone, nor is it one we engage in without hope or joy. We press on because we know that the God who began a good work in us will carry it on to completion (Philippians 1:6). We press on because we know that the battle is already won—Jesus has conquered sin and death. And we press on with joy because we know that in Christ, our victory is secure.

Never give up on the fight for faith. With each step, each trial, and each victory, you are becoming more like Christ, and there is no greater joy than that.

> **JOY BUILDER TIP:**
>
> If not already ask how you can serve at your local church. Find something you are truly passionate about or something that makes you angry in a godly way. Like helping fight against some injustices in the world and please make sure to do it in a biblical way!

CHAPTER 24

I WILL FEAR NO EVIL GOD IS WITH ME

Even though I walk through the valley of the shadow of death, I will fear no evil, for you are with me; your rod and your staff, they comfort me.
Psalm 23:4

> Although we may not always feel His presence. That does "not" mean He is not there.

As we come to the closing chapters of finding joy in Jesus. This is one of the most if not most important truths not only in this book, but in The Bible itself. As a believer no matter how hard things get or how horrible our circumstances may be. This will always remain true. The Creator of the Universe is always with you! He is with you right now brave warrior. Although we may not always feel His presence. That does "not" mean He is not there.

Just like God spoke to Joshua after Moses death. This is a promise that I beseech to mull over and over and speak it out through any trial you face or even when times are good.

"As I was with Moses, so I will be with you; I will never leave you nor forsake you. Be strong and courageous, because you will lead these people to inherit the land I swore to their ancestors to give them."
Joshua 1:5-9

> As He Was With Moses So He Will Be With You

So when you hear that negative doctors report. Fight back and say

"as He was with Moses so He will be with me".

When you feel like you have nothing left to live for and you are tired of the struggle . Remind yourself

"As He was with Moses So He is with me".

Even when death itself comes staring you right in the face it won't matter because

"As He was with Moses So He Will Be With you"

> You have the same power inside you that raised Jesus from the dead!

Please don't let the devil win one more moment of your life. This fight for the joy of Jesus is certainly not an easy one. But you are never alone brave warrior. Because greater is He who is in you than he who is in the world. Please also remind yourself of this truth until it sits deep down in your heart and overflows to anyone who comes near. You have the same power inside you that raised Jesus from the dead! So when you really think about it we truly have nothing to fear. Through Christ even death has no hold on us!

For to me, to live is Christ and to die is gain

Phillipians 1:21

No matter where you are at, or what you are doing, there is no mountain to high and no valley so low that. Not life or death can keep you from God and His love being with you.

For I am convinced that neither death nor life, neither angels nor demons,[a] neither the present nor the future, nor any powers, 39 neither height nor depth, nor anything else in all creation, will be able to separate us from the love of God that is in Christ Jesus our Lord.

Romans 8:38-39

> Nothing. Not anyone or anything including yourself even when we miss the mark can keep us away from God's love.

Nothing. Not anyone or anything including yourself even when we miss the mark can keep us away from God's love. And the more we know that and grow in His love the less we will desire to sin. And even when we fall.

If we confess our sins, He is faithful and just to cleanse us from all unrighteousness

1 John 1:9

One of the greatest promises we have in the Bible comes from Deuteronomy 31:8

The LORD himself goes before you and will be with you; he will never leave you nor forsake you. Do not be afraid; do not be discouraged."

What a great promise and even more so what a great God we have!

I'd like to close this chapter with a quote from one of my favorite great saints. The prince of preachers Charles Spurgeon

> From the pit of hell to the heavens in the sky. God is with you and loves you more than you'll ever know!

"God the Father cannot be against us. He is our Father; he cannot be against his own children. He hath chosen us, he will not cast us away; he hath adopted us into his family, he will never discard us; he hath been pleased to ordain us unto eternal life, he will never reverse the decree. "

Amen I say to that! If you have grabbed one point from this chapter or even this whole book let it be that God is with you no matter where you go brave warrior. From the pit of hell to the heavens in the sky. God is with you and loves you more than you'll ever know!

No one will be able to stand against you all the days of your life.

As I was with Moses, so I will be with you; I will never leave you nor forsake you
(Joshua 1:5)

Keep this Book of the Law always on your lips; meditate on it day and night, so that you may be careful to do everything written in it. Then you will be prosperous and successful. 9 Have I not commanded you? Be strong and courageous. Do not be afraid; do not be discouraged, for the Lord your God will be with you wherever you go."

Joshua 1:8-9

JOY BUILDER TIP:

As you go on through your day, any time you are met with a challenge or just in general say to yourself "As You(God) were with Moses so you will be with me"

CHAPTER 25

REJOICE! AGAIN I SAY REJOICE!

> *Rejoice in the Lord always. I will say it again: Rejoice! 5 Let your gentleness be evident to all. The Lord is near.*
> **Phillipians 4:4-5**

There are certain phrases in life that, when spoken, hold the power to shift the atmosphere around us. "Rejoice, again I say rejoice," is one of those phrases—words that, when repeated, begin to build momentum in the heart and mind of anyone willing to listen. In the case of the apostle Paul, these words were not spoken from a mountaintop of success or wealth but from the very depths of prison. They were not written in a place of comfort but in the midst of personal trials, persecution, and hardship.

Yet, despite these external circumstances, Paul's message remains consistent and clear: Rejoice. Not once, not in passing, but twice, with an emphasis on the certainty of joy found in the Lord. He wasn't suggesting that we rejoice in our suffering, or that joy is to be found in difficult situations for the sake of difficulty itself. No, Paul was pointing to something far deeper: joy as an act of faith and trust in God, irrespective of the circumstances.

REJOICING IN THE LORD

To understand this command, it is essential to grasp the object of our rejoicing. Paul says, "Rejoice in the Lord." It is not "rejoice in your circumstances" or "rejoice in your feelings" or even "rejoice in your achievements" that Paul commands. Instead, he anchors our joy in the Lord—our unshakable, unchanging, all-sufficient God. This is a radical redefinition of joy. It's not about what happens to us or around us, but about who we belong to.

When we rejoice in the Lord, we are affirming that His love, grace, and presence are greater than anything else. The world may shift beneath us, our health may fail, our plans may fall apart, but none of those things can take away the joy that is rooted in Him. To rejoice in the Lord is to say, "Regardless of the storm, God is good, and He is with me."

This is the key to Paul's joy. His circumstances were dire, but he had a relationship with Christ that no prison bars could diminish. When our joy is rooted in the Lord, we are free from the fluctuating emotions that come with our ever-changing environment.

THE POWER OF REPETITION

Paul doesn't merely suggest that we rejoice once; he says, "Rejoice... again I say rejoice." Why the repetition? Paul understood something profound: we need reminders. Our natural tendency is to become focused on what's going wrong in our lives—the lack of money, the struggles at work, the burdens of personal relationships. We fixate on the negative, which drains our energy and our peace.

By saying "Rejoice... again," Paul is drawing our attention away from the natural human inclination to dwell on the negative and refocusing it on God. In a sense, he's giving us a spiritual exercise, one that requires discipline and intention. It's easy to forget joy when we're overwhelmed. It's easy to lose sight of the bigger picture when we're consumed with the immediate. But the act of choosing joy, over and over again, slowly rewires our hearts and minds to trust God in all circumstances.

In his letter to the Philippians, Paul was calling the church to a deeper awareness of God's presence and goodness in every moment. Joy is a choice—a choice we must make, especially when life feels heavy. To rejoice isn't to ignore the difficulties, but to choose to elevate God above them.

A JOY THAT IS NOT CIRCUMSTANTIAL

The beauty of the command to "rejoice" is that it is not based on our circumstances. Paul didn't say, "Rejoice when everything is going well" or "Rejoice when you get the promotion." Rejoicing in the Lord does not depend on favorable outcomes but on an unwavering faith that God is at work, even when we cannot see it.

This is evident in Paul's life. Though he faced imprisonment, rejection, and eventual martyrdom, he continually chose to rejoice. He understood that the joy of the Lord was not something the world could give or take away. It was his strength.

When we view joy as a response to God's unchanging nature, it becomes a well that we can draw from, no matter how parched we feel. Rejoicing in the Lord is not about denying pain or pretending everything is fine when it isn't; rather, it's about trusting that God's sovereignty and love transcend our present reality.

THE FRUIT OF REJOICING

Rejoicing does more than elevate our spirits—it strengthens our faith. Rejoicing helps us to see the world through the lens of God's goodness, even in the hardest of times. It draws us closer to the Lord because joy shifts our perspective from what's wrong to what's right with God.

The act of rejoicing also draws others In. When Paul wrote his letter from prison, his joy became a testimony to the believers around him. He wasn't only writing to encourage himself but to lift the spirits of the Philippians, reminding them that joy was possible, even in their own trials.

As believers, our joy is a powerful witness to a world that is often drowning in sorrow and hopelessness. When we rejoice in the Lord, we reflect the light of Christ, showing the world that there is a joy that transcends anything this world can offer.

REJOICE ALWAYS

"Rejoice in the Lord always," Paul says. The word "always" is an invitation to make joy a constant part of our lives. It's not just for the good days or the days when everything feels easy—it's for the difficult moments too. Rejoicing isn't dependent on the scale of our troubles, but on the certainty of God's character.

As we meditate on Paul's words, let us consider the times in our lives when rejoicing felt impossible. What would it look like to choose joy in those moments, to fix our eyes on the Lord rather than our circumstances? Rejoicing in the Lord does not diminish our struggles but strengthens us to face them with the assurance that God is with us.

In moments of sorrow, fear, or frustration, let us take a moment to pause and choose joy—joy not in the situation, but in the Savior who holds us, comforts us, and promises to never leave us. For in His presence is fullness of joy (Psalm 16:11).

> *"Rejoice in the Lord always. Again I say, rejoice!"*

This is not just a command but an invitation—a call to the deepest joy that can only be found in the unshakable, ever-present love of God. Rejoice, always, for He is with us.

JOY BUILDER TIP:

Do one thing today that you have been procrastinating about, even if it's the smallest thing. After of course thank God but also celebrate seriously!

CHAPTER 26

STIR YOURSELF UP WITH THE JOY OF THE LORD

Stir up [rekindle] the gift of God which is in you through the laying on of my hands. For God has not given us a spirit of fear, but of power and of love and of a sound mind"
2 Timothy 1:6-7

INTRODUCTION: THE POWER OF JOY IN THE LIFE OF A BELIEVER

> It is not an ordinary joy, limited to human emotions or external circumstances. Instead, it is a supernatural joy, rooted in God's unchanging nature and promises

The Christian journey is filled with moments of both triumph and challenge. As believers, we know that life will present difficulties, but we also know the incredible power available to us in the joy of the Lord. It is not an ordinary joy, limited to human emotions or external circumstances. Instead, it is a supernatural joy, rooted in God's unchanging nature and promises. This joy is one of the fruits of the Spirit (Galatians 5:22) and serves as a source of strength in the life of a believer, as Nehemiah 8:10 reminds us:

> *"The joy of the Lord is your strength."*

But how do we maintain that joy? How do we stir ourselves up in it, especially when faced with discouragement, fatigue, or trials? This chapter explores the importance of actively stirring yourself up in the joy of the Lord and provides practical steps to cultivate and maintain it in your daily walk.

THE SOURCE OF JOY: KNOWING GOD AND HIS PROMISES

> When we comprehend that we are loved, forgiven, and adopted into His family, we experience a deep, abiding joy that the world cannot take away.

The foundation of joy lies in our relationship with God. To stir up the joy of the Lord, we must first understand its source: it comes from knowing who God is and standing firm in His promises. When we comprehend that we are loved, forgiven, and adopted into His family, we experience a deep, abiding joy that the world cannot take away.

> True joy is found when we immerse ourselves in God's presence, meditate on His Word, and remember the magnitude of His love.

David, in the Psalms, often spoke of finding joy in God's presence. Psalm 16:11 says,

> *"You make known to me the path of life; in your presence there is fullness of joy; at your right hand are pleasures forevermore."*

True joy is found when we immerse ourselves in God's presence, meditate on His Word, and remember the magnitude of His love.

This joy isn't dependent on circumstances. It's possible to face sorrow, pain, or trials and still have an underlying joy because it springs from the eternal truths of God's faithfulness. Paul exemplified this when he wrote the letter to the Philippians from a prison cell, encouraging believers to

> *"Rejoice in the Lord always"*

(Philippians 4:4). His joy was not based on his circumstances but on the unshakeable reality of his relationship with God.

THE NEED TO STIR YOURSELF UP

Although the joy of the Lord is available to every believer, there are times when we may not feel joyful. Life's demands, challenges, and disappointments can weigh heavily on us, causing us to lose sight of the joy we have in Christ. This is why it's essential to stir ourselves up, to actively remind ourselves of God's goodness, and to reignite that joy.

> This is why it's essential to stir ourselves up, to actively remind ourselves of God's goodness, and to reignite that joy.

In 2 Timothy 1:6, Paul urged Timothy to

> *"fan into flame the gift of God."*

Although he was referring to Timothy's spiritual gifting, the principle applies to our joy as well. We must continually fan the flame of joy so that it burns brightly in our hearts. Like a fire that needs tending, joy requires intentionality—it does not stay vibrant on its own.

PRACTICAL WAYS TO STIR UP THE JOY OF THE LORD

1. Meditate on the Word of God

> Joy flows from a deep connection to God's Word

Joy flows from a deep connection to God's Word. The Bible is filled with promises that remind us of God's goodness, His love for us, and His ultimate victory. When we meditate on the Word, we fill our hearts with truth, and that truth brings joy. Psalm 19:8 declares,

"The precepts of the Lord are right, giving joy to the heart."

Spending time reading, studying, and meditating on Scripture allows God's promises to take root in our hearts and awaken joy.

2. Worship and Praise

> When we praise God, we shift our focus from our problems to His greatness.

Worship is a powerful way to stir up joy. When we praise God, we shift our focus from our problems to His greatness. In Psalm 100:4, we are instructed to

"Enter His gates with thanksgiving and His courts with praise."

Praise opens the door to joy because it reminds us of who God is and all that He has done for us. Worship shifts the atmosphere, lifting our spirits as we declare God's goodness.

3. Gratitude

> Gratitude transforms our outlook, helping us see God's hand in every situation.

A heart of gratitude fuels joy. When we intentionally focus on what we are thankful for, it realigns our perspective and stirs up joy. Philippians 4:6-7 encourages us to present our requests to God with thanksgiving, promising that His peace will guard our hearts. Gratitude transforms our outlook, helping us see God's hand in every situation.

4. Prayer and Communion with God

> Prayer is a direct Invitation to experience the fullness of joy that comes from communion with God.

Spending time in prayer is another way to stir up joy. Prayer is a conversation with God, and through it, we pour out our hearts, share our burdens, and receive His peace. In His presence, we are refreshed and renewed, and joy naturally follows. In John 16:24, Jesus said,

"Ask, and you will receive, that your joy may be full."

Prayer is a direct Invitation to experience the fullness of joy that comes from communion with God.

5. Surround Yourself with Other Believers

Joy can often be rekindled in community. Hebrews 10:24-25 urges us not to forsake gathering together because fellowship encourages us. Being around other believers who share our faith uplifts our spirits, and their joy can inspire and ignite our own. Sharing testimonies, praying together, and simply enjoying fellowship with others reminds us that we are part of a greater body of Christ, united in His love.

6. Serve Others

> When we take our focus off ourselves and help meet the needs of others, we reflect the heart of Christ.

Serving others can often stir up joy in our hearts. When we take our focus off ourselves and help meet the needs of others, we reflect the heart of Christ. Acts 20:35 tells us,

"It is more blessed to give than to receive."

As we serve, we experience the joy that comes from living out our faith in tangible ways.

MAINTAINING JOY THROUGH TRIALS

> This may seem counterintuitive, but joy in trials is possible because we know God is working for our good, even in difficulty.

One of the greatest tests of joy comes during trials. James 1:2-3 tells us,

"Consider it pure joy, my brothers and sisters, whenever you face trials of many kinds, because you know that the testing of your faith produces perseverance."

This may seem counterintuitive, but joy in trials is possible because we know God is working for our good, even in difficulty.

When faced with hardship, we can choose joy by trusting in God's sovereignty and goodness. Trials develop perseverance and deepen our faith. They remind us that our ultimate hope is not in this world but in God's eternal kingdom.

CONCLUSION: JOY AS A STRENGTH AND A TESTIMONY

> When the world sees us walking in joy despite challenges, it points them to the source of our joy—Jesus Christ.

As we stir ourselves up in the joy of the Lord, we find strength for every season of life. Joy is not only a source of personal empowerment; it is also a testimony to others. When the world sees us walking in joy despite challenges, it points them to the source of our joy—Jesus Christ.

Stirring up the joy of the Lord is an ongoing process, one that requires intentionality and faith. But as we cultivate joy, we will experience the fullness of life that Jesus promised and live out the vibrant testimony of His transforming power in us.

JOY BUILDER TIP:
Find and watch a godly movie with someone you love. There are a lot of great ones. But I recommend the passion of Christ. I know it is sometimes heartbreaking to watch. But if you do choose it as our great Lord endures the worst suffering ever, keep in mind He did that for you!

CHAPTER 27

I CAN DO ALL THINGS THROUGH CHRIST

Not that I speak in regard to need, for I have learned in whatever state I am, to be content: I know how to [a]be abased, and I know how to [b]abound. Everywhere and in all things I have learned both to be full and to be hungry, both to abound and to suffer need. I can do all things through [c]Christ who strengthens me.
Philippians 4:11-13

As we start off this chapter and this verse , it is very important to know that the apostle Paul was not writing this letter in some high rise apartment and definitely not on some vacation by the sea. But he wrote this letter while other than hell and being stuck your mind, in probably the worst place possible. A Roman dungeon or jail. When you have that knowledge and then look at the verse again, you might think Paul is a little crazy. And personally I kind of believe he was but in a God way. The book of Phillipians is most noted as a treatise on joy. How on earth or in heaven was Paul able to not only think of himself less but even more so , he wrote this to stir up joy in his fellow believers! I don't know about you guys, but if I was sitting in a dungeon basically by myself , joy would probably be the furthest thought and topic away from me. But knowing what we know now let us discover how we can have that same joy in any circumstance. Even in our own dungeons.

As we notice from the verse at the beginning of this chapter, this did not happen overnight for Paul. He said he "learned" how to be content. As I was preparing for this chapter I searched for some biblical commentary on this section and here is something I found from bibleref.com

"Paul was able to find joy in his circumstances, even when he was in prison, because he had learned how to be content. Contentment is not a natural attitude, but rather a skill that can be learned. Contentment means wanting what God wants for us, rather than what we want for ourselves. " I love that. Contentment is what God wants for us rather than what we want for ourselves. And the real truth is that what God wants for us is eternally better than anything we could ever come up with. As Jeremiah 29:11

Says "For I know the plans I have for you,' declares the Lord, 'plans to prosper you and not to harm you, plans to give you a hope and a future. '" if we are being honest most of our wants only get us in more trouble. But when we want God above all else there is no trouble we cannot face and overcome. Joy and love are not just butterfly stomach feelings. They can definitely bring that. But it is far deeper and more beautiful than that sensation. As we know from Apostle Paul in 1 Corinthians 13. Love is greater than anything. We also know God is love and just. But as love pertains to joy. There would be no joy without love and there would certainly be no love or for that matter there would be no anything without God. If you want to increase your joy, then live in the love of God. Love bears all things, believes all things, hopes all things, endures all things." 1 Corinthians 13:7

So why did Paul have joy in one of the worst possible circumstances? Because he knew without a shadow of doubt that he was loved eternally by our great Lord.

Paul endured more than most ever have in 2 Corinthians 11:23-29 he shares his sufferings

Are they servants of Christ? (I am out of my mind to talk like this.) I am more. I have worked much harder, been in prison more frequently, been flogged more severely, and been exposed to death again and again. 24 Five times I received from the Jews the forty lashes minus one. 25 Three times I was beaten with rods, once I was pelted with stones, three times I was shipwrecked, I spent a night and a day in the open sea, 26 I have been constantly on the move. I have been in danger from rivers, in danger from bandits, in danger from my fellow Jews, in danger from Gentiles; in danger in the city, in danger in the country, in danger at sea; and in danger from false believers. 27 I have labored and toiled and have often gone without sleep; I have known hunger and thirst and have often gone without food; I have been cold and naked. 28 Besides everything else, I face daily the pressure of my concern for all the churches.

Look at the beginning of verse 23. I told you Paul was crazy! But again in a godly way.

And Paul goes onto say in Phillipians 3:8-9

Yes, everything else is worthless when compared with the infinite value of knowing Christ Jesus my Lord. For his sake I have discarded everything else, counting it all as garbage, so that I could gain Christ and become one with him.

The KJV translation says he counted everything as dung. I am not even going to say the word that most of us would translate it to in English. But you get the idea. So what was it or should I say Who was that Paul found joy in any predicament he was in? It was knowing Christ. And more importantly being known and eternally loved by Christ. Pull knew deep within that no matter where he was or what came against him. That his relationship with Jesus was far greater than anything this world can offer. Actually far greater than anything in general. Whether life or death if you believe you are in Christ mighty warrior and that will literally save you from the depths of hell!

> For to me, to live is Christ [He is my source of joy, my reason to live] and to die is gain [for I will be with Him in eternity]. Phillipians 1:21 Amp

I ask this with all love in my heart and ask myself the same question. What "dung" is it that you may be holding onto that seems impossible to let go. And if you are being honest you know that is not truly bringing you joy. Maybe it did for a season. But it is only in Christ that we can have joy forevermore. I beseech you with all that is in me that you go to the Father with this dung. If it was sinful of course let us confess. Let us give it all to Him and keep it with Him. And most importantly we must ask Him to forgive us for putting anything ahead of Him and ask Him that your heart puts Him in the only place he deserves and that is number one! Though it definitely grieves the Father and Holy Spirit when we don't put them first. God is not disappointed with you. Nor is He surprised. He knows everything from start to finish and eternally more. But when He knows that you want to want Him. He finds great joy in His children loving Him.

> *You will seek me and find me when you seek me with all your heart.*
> ***Jeremiah 29:13***

As we end this chapter, I pray with all that is within me, that like Paul in prison , that you can truly have the joy and peace in any circumstance that comes your way. And never forget, you can do all things that Christ strengthens you to do!

I'd like to end this chapter with a commentary from Ellicots

I can do all things.—Properly, I have strength in all things, rather (according to the context) to bear than to do. But the universal extension of the maxim beyond the immediate occasion and context is not inadmissible. It represents the ultimate and ideal consciousness of the Christian. The first thing needful is to throw off mere self-sufficiency, to know our weakness and sin, and accept the salvation of God's free grace in Christ; the next, to find the "strength made perfect in weakness," and in that to be strong.

> **JOY BUILDER TIP:**
>
> If you don't already have one or you have been using the same one for a while. Find yourself a biblical awesome devotional. I highly recommend anything from Charles Stanley or Charles Spurgeoun.

CHAPTER 28
ETERNAL JOY

You have made it to the end of the book! You truly are a brave warrior. But your walk with joy has truly just begun!

I pray with all my heart that you apply The principles you have learned here by applying The Word of God to your life.

It's time to tell the devil that through Christ, His Word with the Joy Of Jesus Himself. That today is the day that he will win no more. It's time to finally silence the lies of satan, the world and the flesh and live in Joy like never before. So we can truly live out the great commission that our Lord has set before us! Please don't take one more day of the attacks of the devil and his demonic cohorts. Through Christ you are more than a conquer and I know somewhere deep inside you know you were created for so much more. And you were. I pray with all that is in me that this book through the words of God, helps stir up that flame and passion within so you can live and love like never before! That no matter where you have been or no matter where you are going. You are loved by the King Of Kings. That you are never alone. That today is the day you decide to finally live in the joy of the Lord and never look back! Please don't let the devil or anyone steal one more second from your life. Just like our great Lord did in the wilderness, fight back the powers of hell with The Word of God. And never forget that the joy of the Lord is your strength! You got this brave warrior! God is with you and will always be with you. Fear not and never turn back decide to live in the joy of Jesus this moment until you meet him face to face! And

May the God of hope fill you with all joy and peace in believing, so that by the power of the Holy Spirit you may abound in hope Romans 15:13

CONCLUSION

THE JOY OF JESUS - CRUSHING ALL OTHER IDOLS

In this final chapter, we come full circle, contemplating the overwhelming joy found in Jesus and the decisive choice we make to reject every competing idol. In a world filled with endless voices promising fulfillment, peace, and satisfaction, we have uncovered the deep truth: there is no greater joy than knowing, loving, and following Jesus Christ. The life that seeks Him alone, forsaking all other idols, finds a joy that is not circumstantial but eternal.

Throughout this journey, we have seen the subtle yet persistent ways idols attempt to stake claims on our hearts. Wealth, status, relationships, comfort, and even our own plans and ambitions—all can become idols that challenge our devotion to Christ. Each idol, though often harmless in its origin, takes on a life of its own when it begins to overshadow our relationship with Jesus. We can now see how these idols, if left unchecked, demand our allegiance and distort our joy, creating a counterfeit version of the fulfillment only Jesus provides.

But Jesus came to set us free, not only from the penalty of sin but also from every force that would try to entrap us and rob us of our joy in Him. His love and grace empower us to recognize and dismantle these idols, tearing down anything that stands in the way of a pure and vibrant relationship with Him. The joy we find in Jesus is not a superficial happiness, but a profound contentment and peace that persists through every season of life.

As we conclude, we are called to live in the freedom that comes from loving Jesus above all else. We are invited to surrender daily, letting go of anything that competes for our affections and allowing Christ to fill us with His Spirit. This daily surrender is not a loss but a gain, as it deepens our experience of His love and strengthens our resolve to keep Him at the center of our lives.

Let us leave behind the empty promises of idols and press on to experience the fullness of joy found in Jesus. By crushing these idols and choosing Him, we embrace a life marked by purpose, peace, and true fulfillment. With each passing day, may our hearts grow more captivated by the love of Christ, until His joy becomes our ultimate treasure and our lasting reward.

In the end, the choice is ours. Jesus offers Himself fully to us, and in Him, we find everything we could ever hope for. The idols may call, but we know now who holds our hearts. So let us joyfully say, "Yes, Lord, I choose You." And in that choice, we discover the joy of Jesus—a joy that is indeed worth everything.

Made in the USA
Monee, IL
11 January 2025